HOW TO DRAW MANGA

POCKET SIZED! with BEN DUNN DAVID HUTCHISON and ROD ESPINOSA

With Additional text by ROBERT ACOSTA

Antarctic Press Presents: *How to Draw Manga Pocket Manga* Vol. 3, February 2008, is published by Antarctic Press, 72 Wurzbach, Suite #204, San Antonio, Texas, 78240. FAX#: (210) 614-5029. Text ©2008 Robert Acosta & David Hutchison. Art ©2008 Ben Dunn, David Hutchison & Rod Espinosa. All other material is ™ and ©2008 Antarctic Press. No similarity to any actual person(s) and/or place(s) is intended, and any such similarity is entirely coincidental. Nothing from this book may be reproduced without the express written consent of the authors, except for purposes of review or promotion. "let you talk the geek-talk to him." Printed and bound in Canada by Imprimerie Lebonfon, Inc.

For more great "How to DRAW" merchandise, go to:

www.APMANGA.com

Drawing the Figure

Picking up where we left off last time, we continue our lessons in drawing the wide variety of shonen manga body archetypes.

The number of manga that contain grandfather- and grandmother-type characters is considerable, and the number of roles they fill equally numerous. Just like the grandfather, the grandmother—or, more precisely, the old woman body type—can be perfectly suited to the role of old, lecherous comic relief. On the other side of the coin, old women can be nurturers who are there to provide advice and progress the story through revelatory exposition.

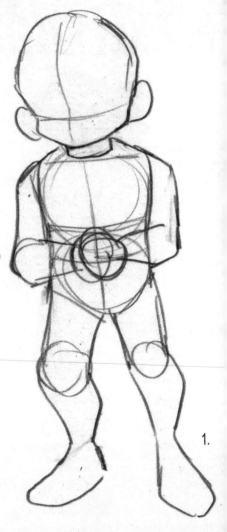

1.

HOW TO DRAW MANGA

Drawing the Figure

2.

Drawing the Figure

3.

Drawing the Figure

4.

HOW TO DRAW MANGA

Drawing the Figure

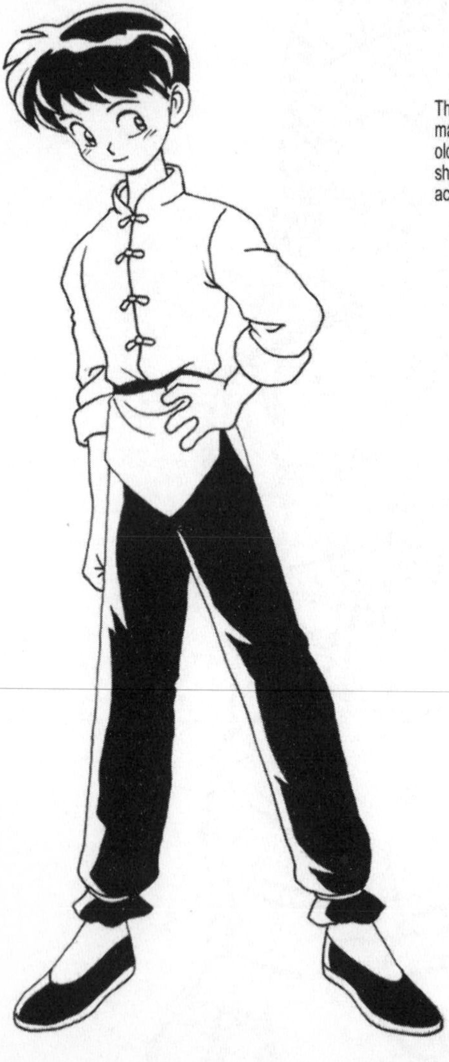

The short stature of this body type makes the character seem frail and older. A good rule of thumb is the shorter and the more wrinkly the character, the older (s)he is.

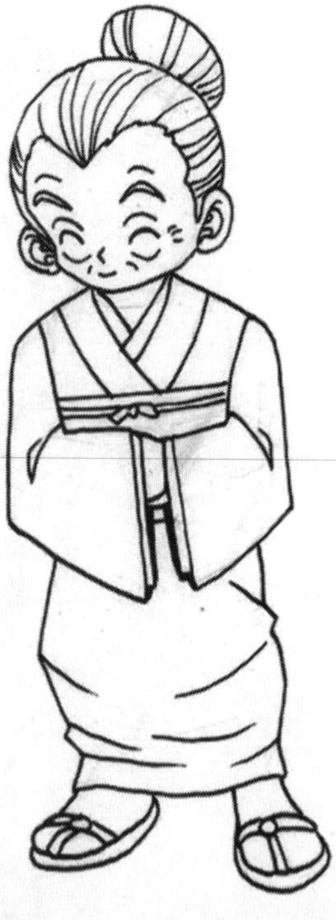

PRACTICE PAGE

HOW TO DRAW MANGA

Drawing the Figure

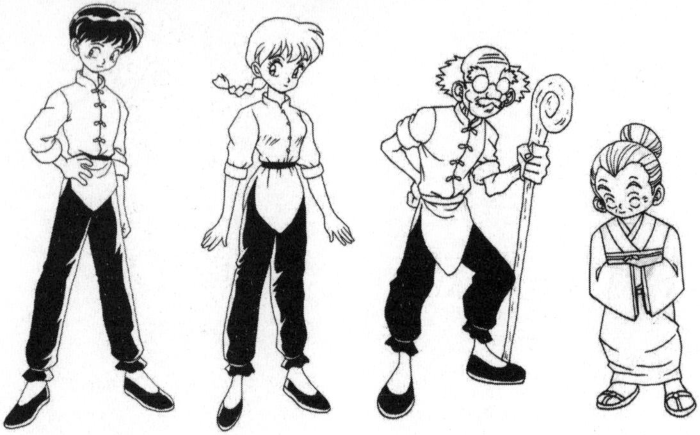

These basic body types are all you will need to make great manga. There are a few others you might want to use, but for your basic stories, you have all you need here. I hope you have begun to get comfortable with these body types, because we are going to be moving ahead full steam from here.

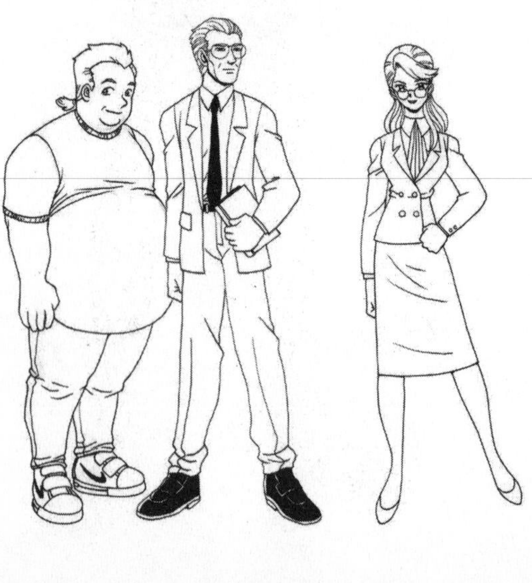

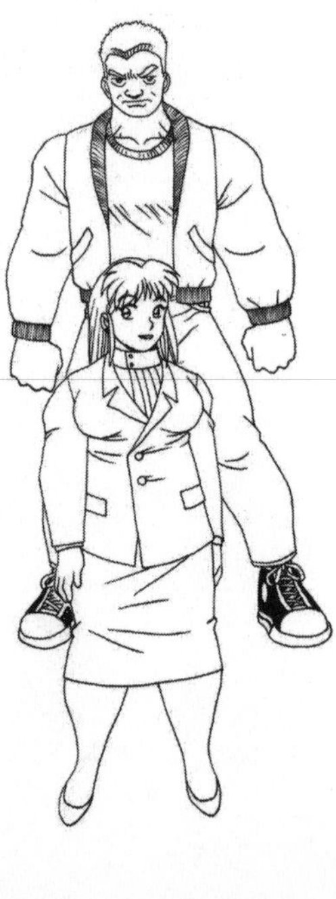

HOW TO DRAW MANGA

Character Design

One of the most fun and also most difficult things in manga is character design. The main reason why is probably because it's really hard to come up with something new that hasn't been seen before. Now that doesn't mean that we, as artists, can't draw our inspiration from other things. In this chapter, we will go over using reference and costume design and how these elements help in developing memorable and, hopefully, original characters. Let's get started!

HOW TO DRAW MANGA

Character Design

Let's warm up with some basics. Remember, when starting an illustration, make sure you lay out the figure using basic shapes.

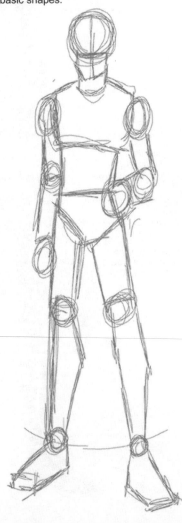

HOW TO DRAW MANGA

Character Design

Then, lightly sketch in the details. Keep in mind that when you draw clothes, make sure that you are including the wrinkles and folds. These details will help not only give the audience an accurate image of the type of clothes the character is wearing, they will also help make your illustration look solid and three-dimensional. In designing characters, personality is a huge factor in what a character wears, how they stand, and how they look overall.

HOW TO DRAW MANGA

Character Design

HOW TO DRAW MANGA
Character Design

Dark colors, and most importantly blacks, send the quickest message to the viewer. When illustrating in blacks, be sure to lay out your highlights in pencil before you go to the inking stage.

PRACTICE PAGE

HOW TO DRAW MANGA

Character Design

Okay, let's design a futuristic space warrior. We start with a pose that would compliment this character: rigid with a wide, balanced stance.

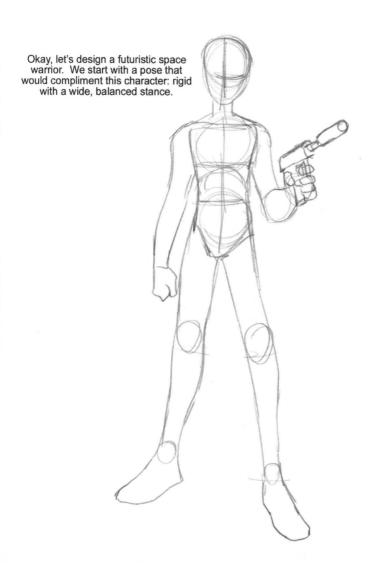

HOW TO DRAW MANGA
Character Design

HOW TO DRAW MANGA

Character Design

Now we need to choose a look for his wardrobe. A good place to start is with uniforms and equipment used by police and soldiers today—in this instance, a helmet, chest armor, and of course, his pistol.

HOW TO DRAW MANGA

Character Design

As you can see, several present-day
elements can be used to influence
your futuristic designs. S.W.A.T.
team uniforms as well as some older
elements were used as a jumping-off
point for this design

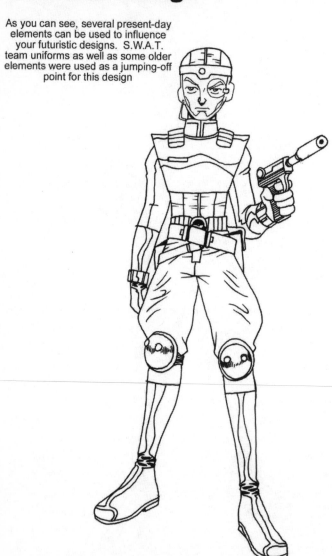

PRACTICE PAGE

Character Design

The design goes a step beyond the inital S.W.A.T. uniform but still keeps some of the same older uniform elements, incorporating these pieces in your design will help keep the uniform believable.

When drawing armor, be sure to draw the armor fitting properly onto the figure. Armor won't sit right against the form, you need to account for the muscles, skin, and clothing under the armor or other

YES   **NO**

And as mentioned before, always try to use reference when you can. It is the easiest and fastest way to get the results you want.

HOW TO DRAW MANGA

Character Design

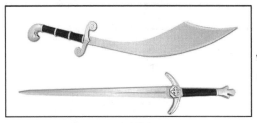

Coming up with new ideas for weapons is again found in the old. Using old swords has helped in coming up with the design for this adventurer's weapon of choice.

Character design isn't only about who they are or what they wear, it's also about things they come in contact with. Accessories and weapons your character uses can speak volumes about who they are and where they've come from.

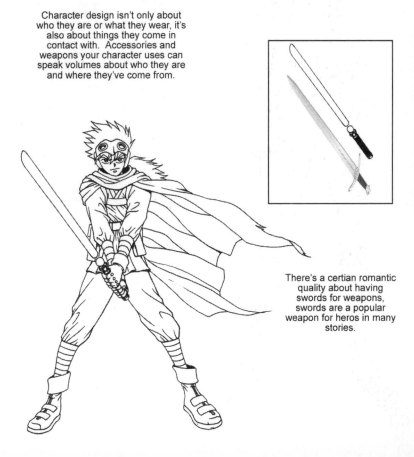

There's a certian romantic quality about having swords for weapons, swords are a popular weapon for heros in many stories.

HOW TO DRAW MANGA

Character Design

Hairstyles are great ways to add personality to a character. The semi-afro is a popular hairstyle coming back into the mainstream, and besides it's fun to draw!

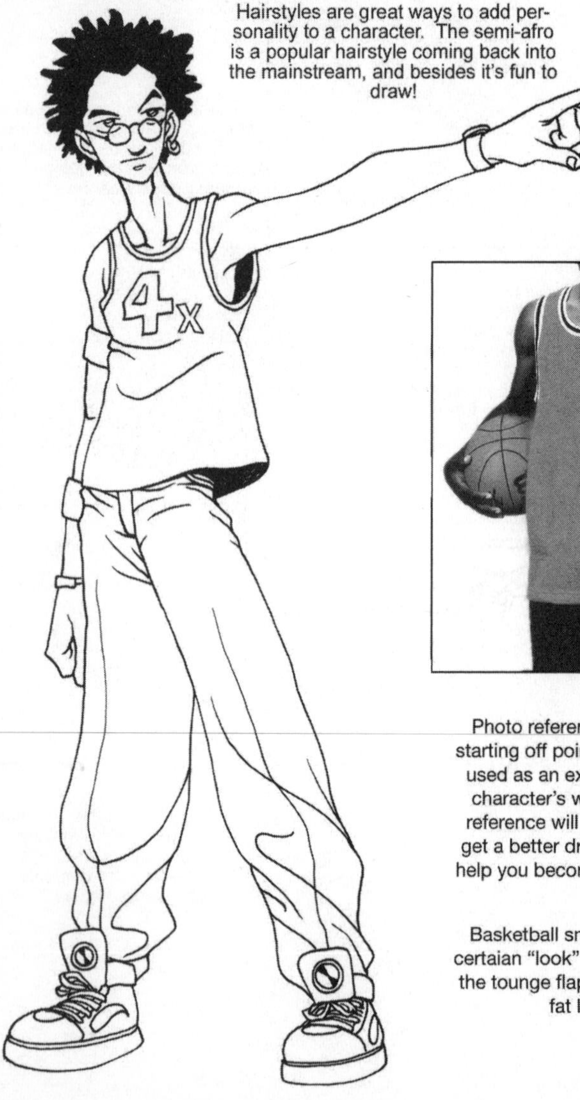

4x

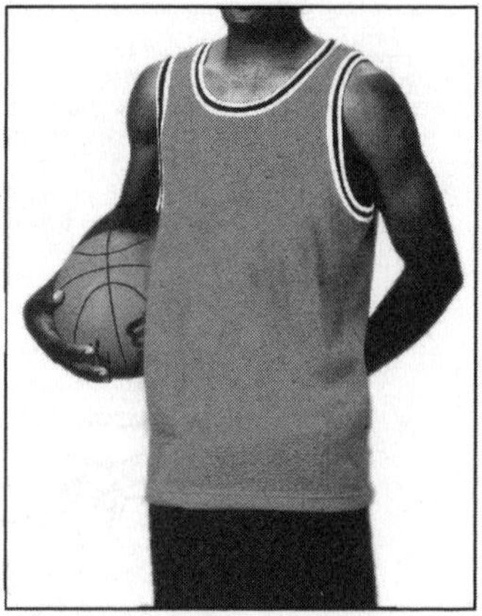

Photo reference is not only a starting off point but can be also used as an exact piece of the character's wardrobe. Using reference will always help you get a better drawing as well as help you become a better artist.

Basketball sneakers have a certaian "look" to them, such as the tounge flap sticking out or fat laces

Character Design

Clothes don't always make the man. When designing characters, body type also says a lot about a character. In the case of these two guys, they're wearing the same outfits, but they are built differently. What personality are you getting from each of them?

The baseball cap is a favorite among the "rebel" types.

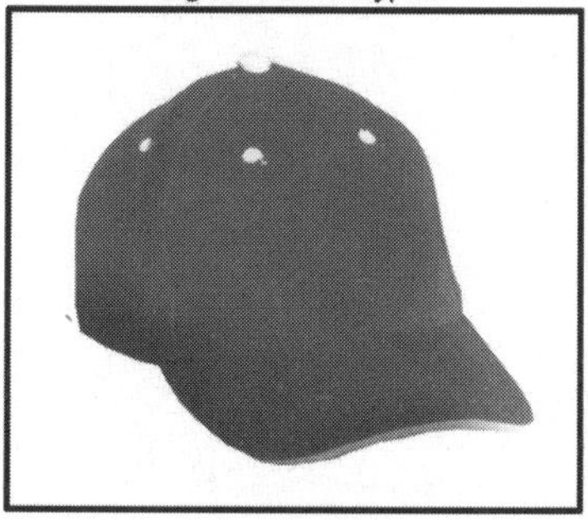

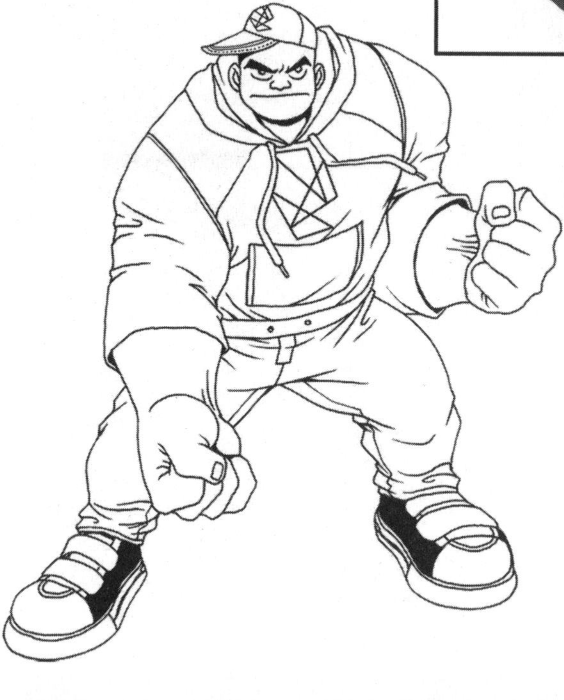

Character Design

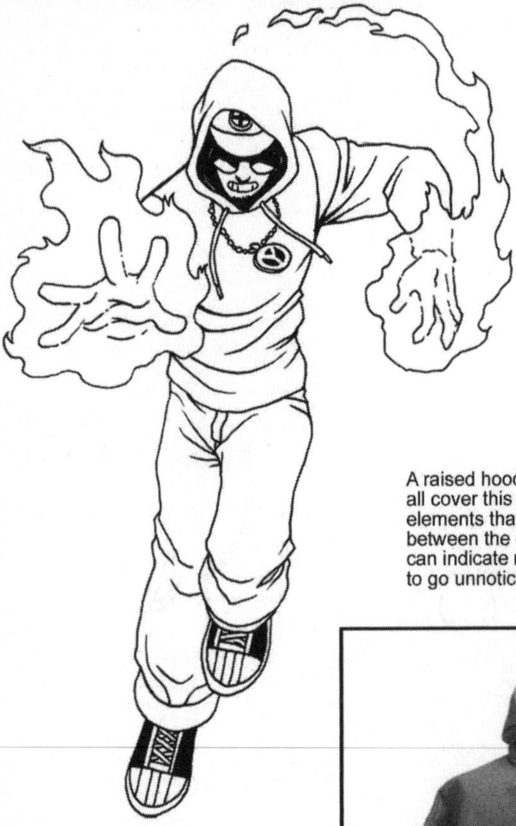

A raised hood, a hat, and sunglasses all cover this character's face. Design elements that create a barrier between the character and the world can indicate many things, like a desire to go unnoticed.

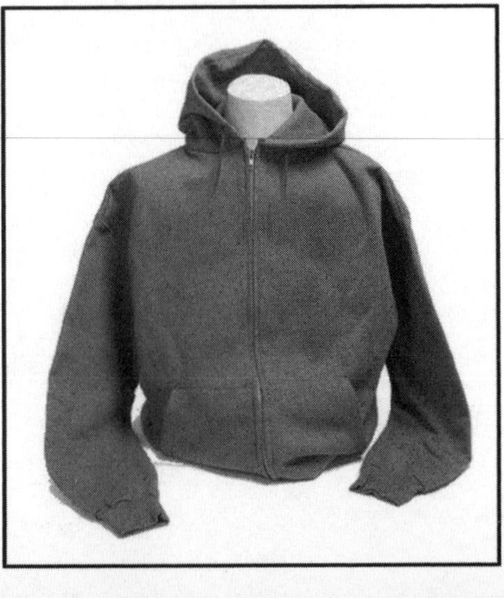

HOW TO DRAW MANGA

Character Design

One of the most successful subgenera of science fiction is that of space battles, usually involving space armadas, space fighters, and often space-worthy robots. The most important element of design in stories like this is how the uniform will look, since most of the characters will be wearing the same thing. You may differentiate between different military divisions and jobs, but the overall design of the uniform is very significant.

A few things that are important on any uniform: what side you're on (the shoulder insignia), who you are (a name tag on the chest), and what your rank is (shoulder tabs).

HOW TO DRAW MANGA
Character Design

The "Rogue Type" character here is wearing high boots, a midriff shirt, and high-cut jacket all complete the roguish look.

The skin-tight outfit is not quite as easy as it may seem. The real trick to it is laying out the highlights on the outfit. A good place to look to for reference is real life. Find a highly reflective material like a shiny plastic cup or patent leather shoes so you can study what light does when it hits it.

HOW TO DRAW MANGA

Character Design

HOW TO DRAW MANGA
Character Design

HOW TO DRAW MANGA

Character Design

The all-black leather outfit is a very popular costume for "edgy" heroines

PRACTICE PAGE

HOW TO DRAW MANGA

Character Design

There are many different types of uniforms that people wear. Look around you and see how people are dressing, and then fast-forward them a couple hundred years.

Adding gloves and boots generally helps enhance a futuristic character's look.

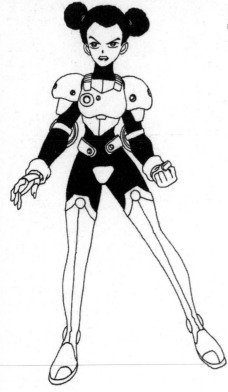

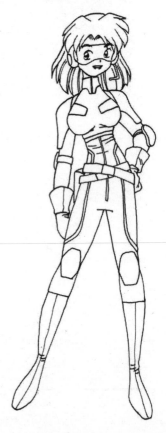

These designs are relatively the same, with just minor differences. As you can see, with small additions and subtractions, there can be several variations on the same line of thinking.

HOW TO DRAW MANGA

Character Design

Drawing cloth properly is almost as important as the figure itself. In this example, you want to treat the cape as a separate shape, almost as a separate character. This approach will help make it easier to draw more convincing capes and clothing.

HOW TO DRAW MANGA

Character Design

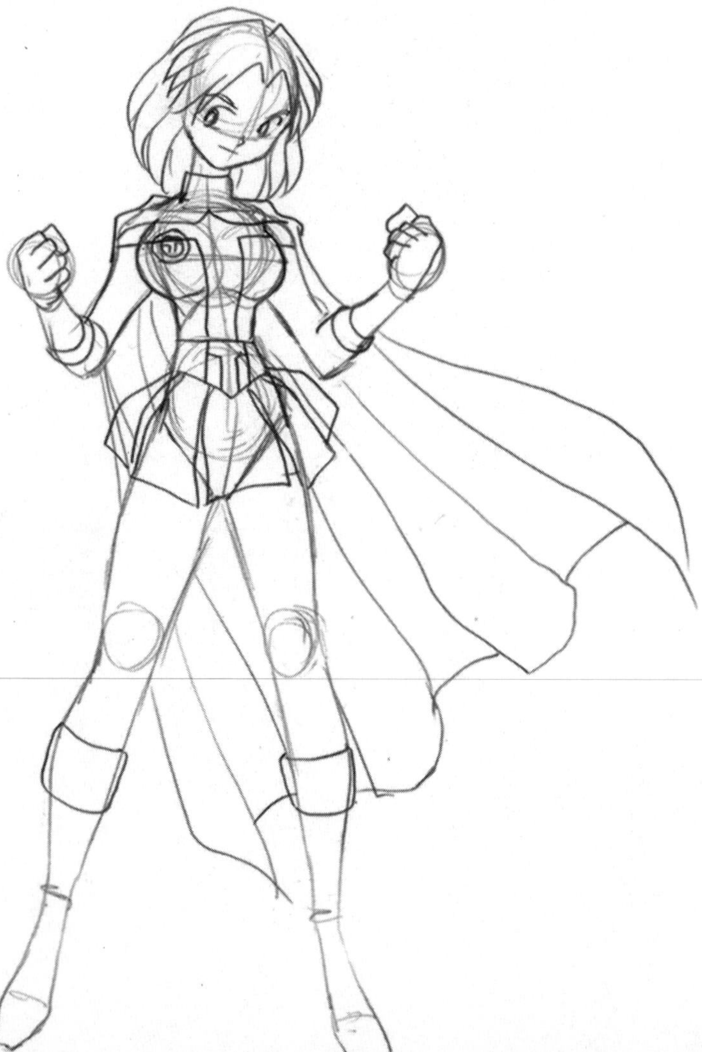

HOW TO DRAW MANGA

Character Design

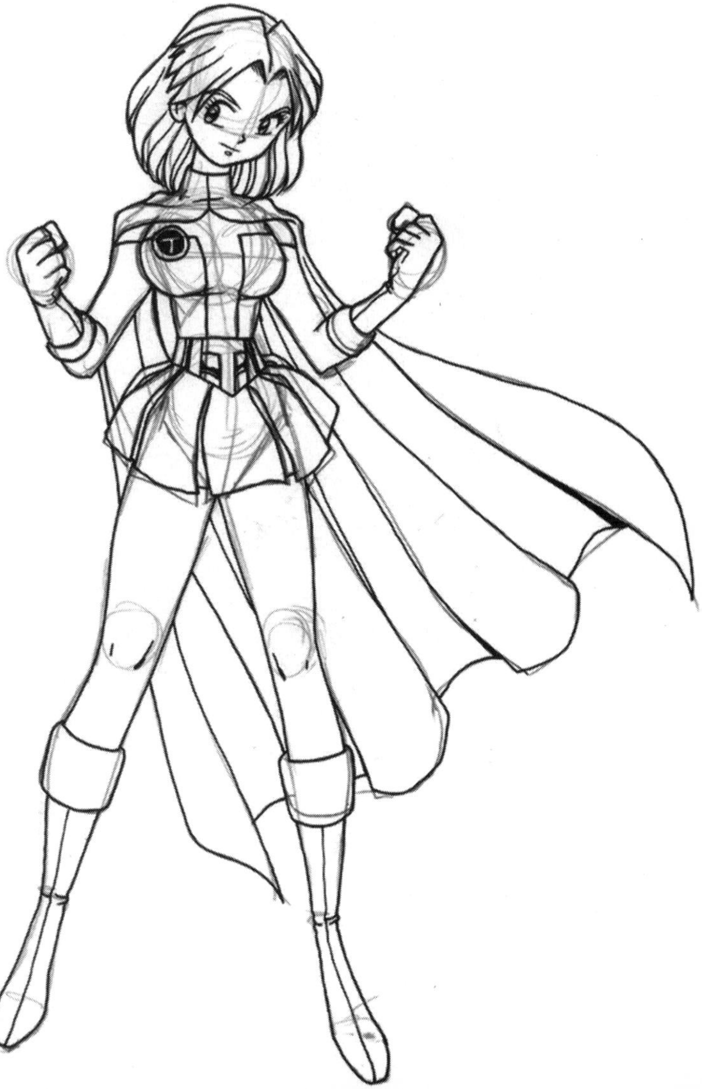

HOW TO DRAW MANGA

Character Design

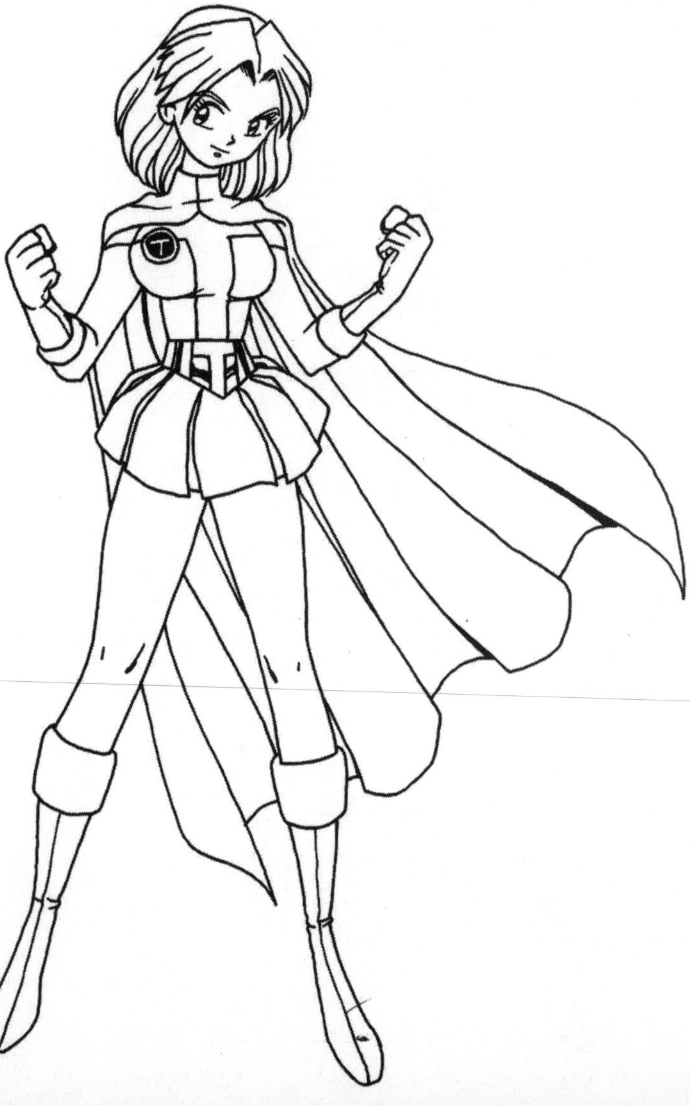

PRACTICE PAGE

Here is an example of lots of cloth. Don't let that affect how you draw your figure. Always start with a light sketch using basic shapes. Then, as you go to the drawing of clothes, remember to draw the clothes flowing around the figure, not clinging to it.

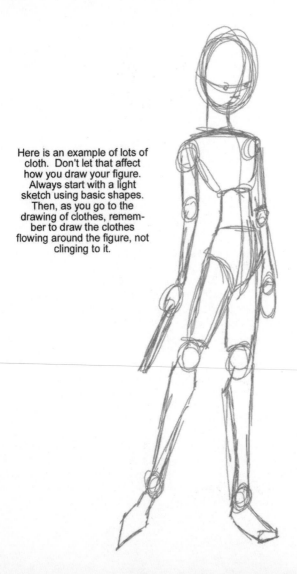

HOW TO DRAW MANGA
Character Design

The tiara signifies royalty, a must for a space princess!

The long, slender pistol reflects the character's slender build.

PRACTICE PAGE

Drawing Villains

Now that you've mastered the basics of drawing and you've been practicing with designing your own heroic characters, it's time to have a little fun. The Bad Guys! Ya love to hate 'em, now let's give designing 'em a try! As you'll see, inspiraion for the bad guys can come from many different people, places and things. Sometimes, even your worst nightmare can be the *best* source for your sinister sketckbook scaries!

So, let's get started!!

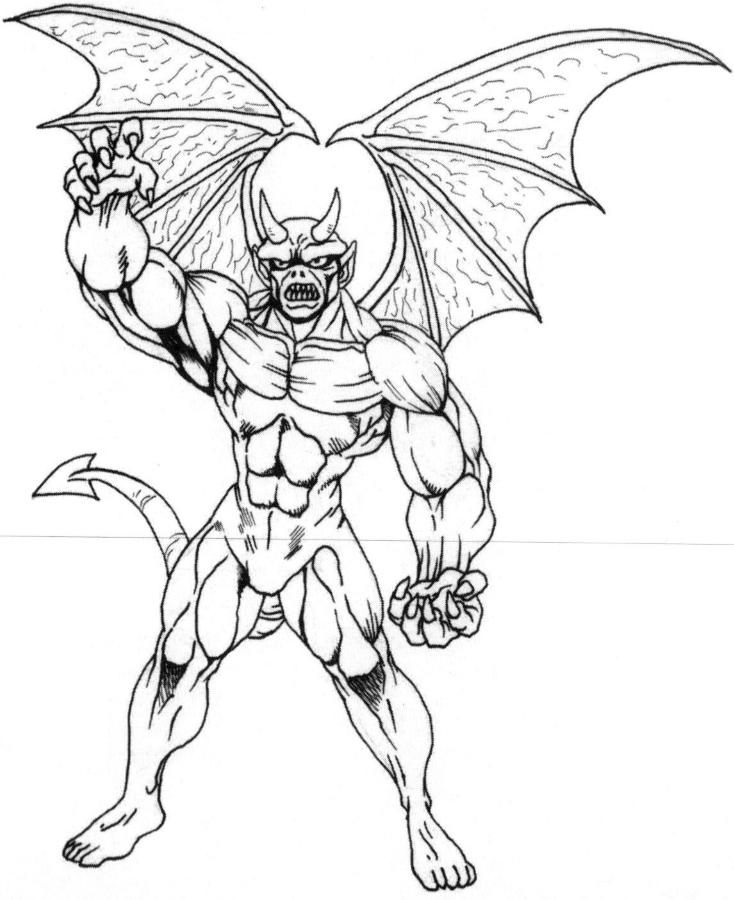

HOW TO DRAW MANGA
Drawing Villains

Let's start with our grumpy pal from the last page.

As always, you want to start every figure with the basic shapes. The proportions of this guy are that of a body-builder.

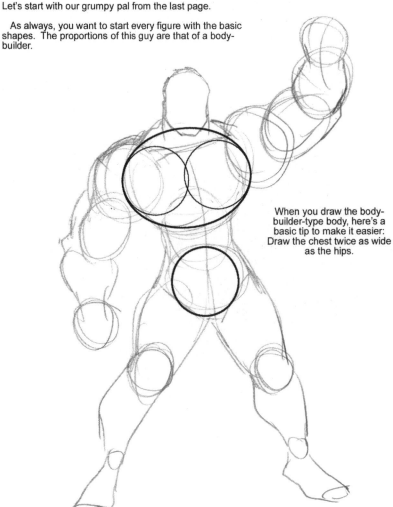

When you draw the body-builder-type body, here's a basic tip to make it easier: Draw the chest twice as wide as the hips.

HOW TO DRAW MANGA

Drawing Villains

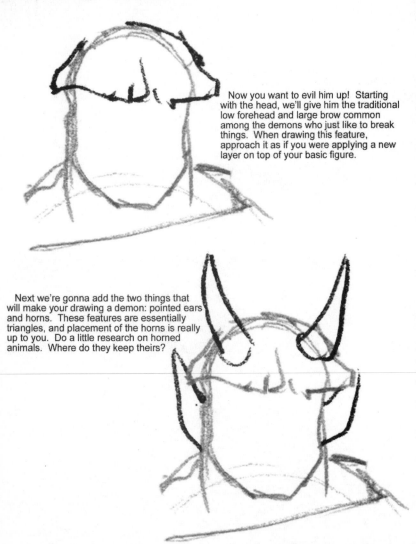

Now you want to evil him up! Starting with the head, we'll give him the traditional low forehead and large brow common among the demons who just like to break things. When drawing this feature, approach it as if you were applying a new layer on top of your basic figure.

Next we're gonna add the two things that will make your drawing a demon: pointed ears and horns. These features are essentially triangles, and placement of the horns is really up to you. Do a little research on horned animals. Where do they keep theirs?

Drawing Villains

Ears, horns and forehead are
done, but we're not through yet!

Drawing Villains

Here's another instance where using reference will help make your drawing realistic and believable. Basing your creations on things that exist in nature is a sure way to attain a believability you wouldn't get otherwise.

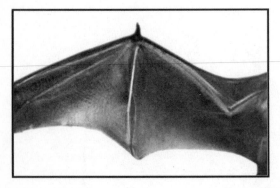

Pay close attention to why things are the way they are, not just how they look. For instance, the bones of the bat wing stretch the loose skin for flight, and if you notice, the bones all meet at one point on the wing.

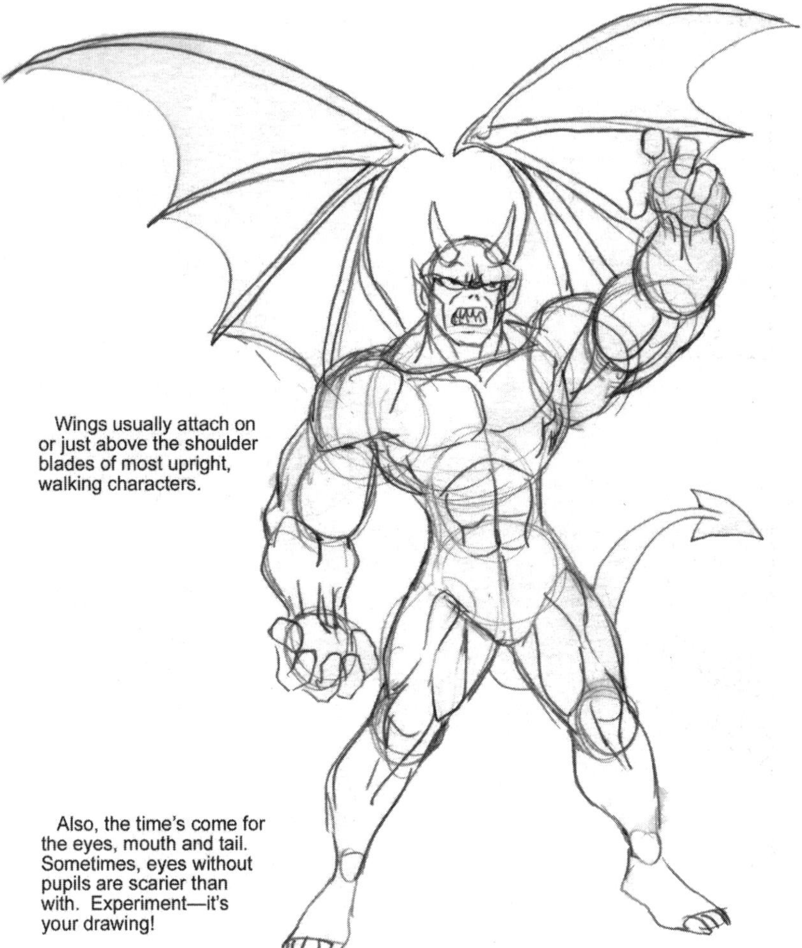

Wings usually attach on or just above the shoulder blades of most upright, walking characters.

Also, the time's come for the eyes, mouth and tail. Sometimes, eyes without pupils are scarier than with. Experiment—it's your drawing!

Drawing Villains

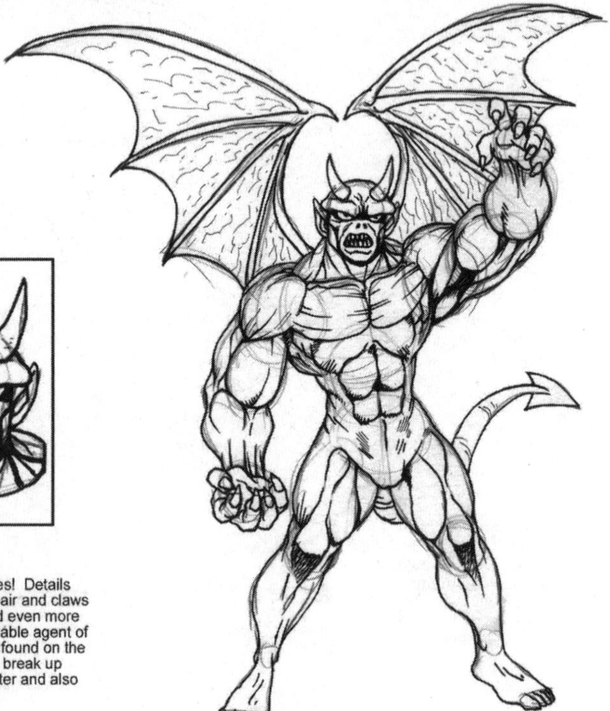

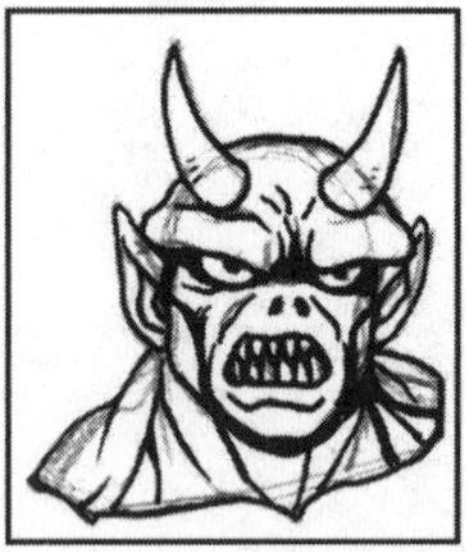

Time for details and textures! Details like black around the eyes, hair and claws are nice touches that will add even more menace to an already formidable agent of evil! And textures like those found on the tail and the skin of the wings break up empty space on your character and also give a little depth and form.

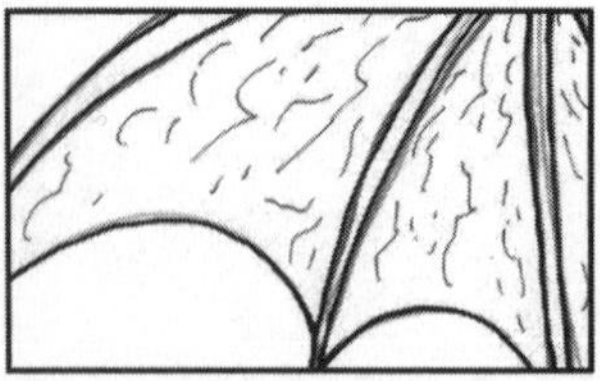

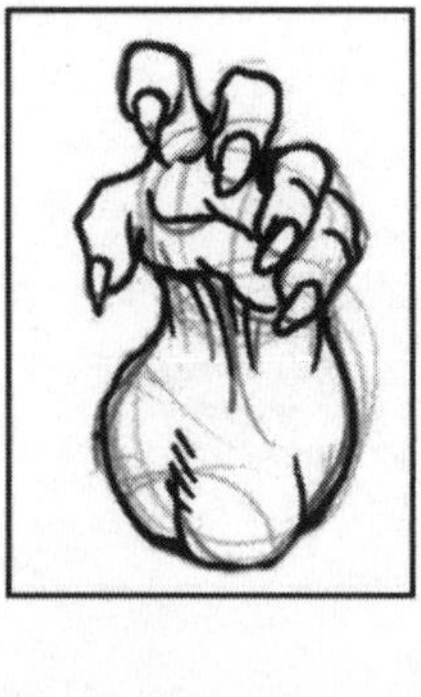

Drawing Villains

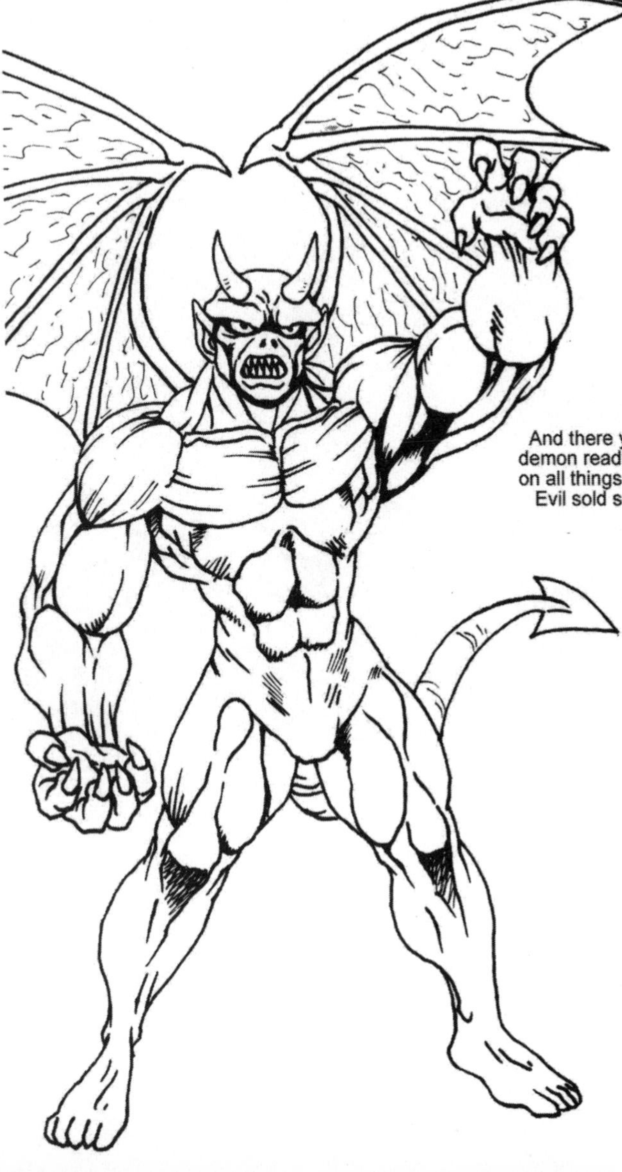

And there you go! A full demon ready to wreak havoc on all things good..
Evil sold seperately...

PRACTICE PAGE

Drawing Villains

What a difference a power tool makes! As shown here, reference has a lot to do with making or breaking this drawing. Getting the hands and arms positioned correctly would be difficult, even for the seasoned artist.

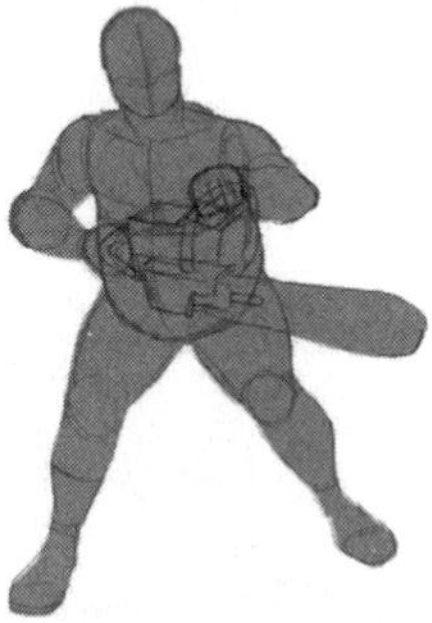

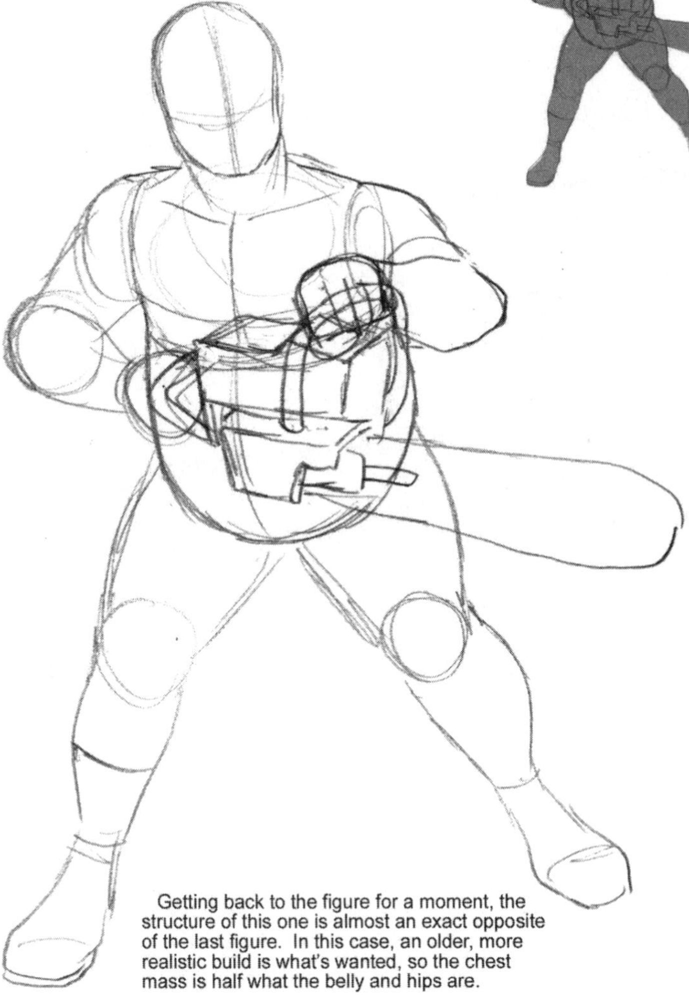

Getting back to the figure for a moment, the structure of this one is almost an exact opposite of the last figure. In this case, an older, more realistic build is what's wanted, so the chest mass is half what the belly and hips are.

HOW TO DRAW MANGA

Drawing Villains

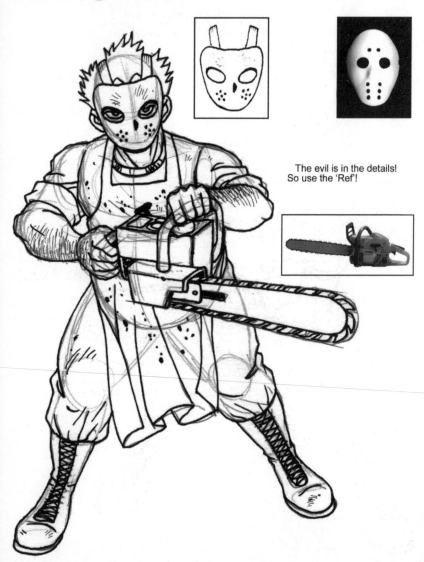

The evil is in the details!
So use the 'Ref'!

Drawing Villains

It's time for the simple little details, like arm hair and splatters of stuff that is hopefully tree sap. Also, you can use this step to clean up your pencil lines.

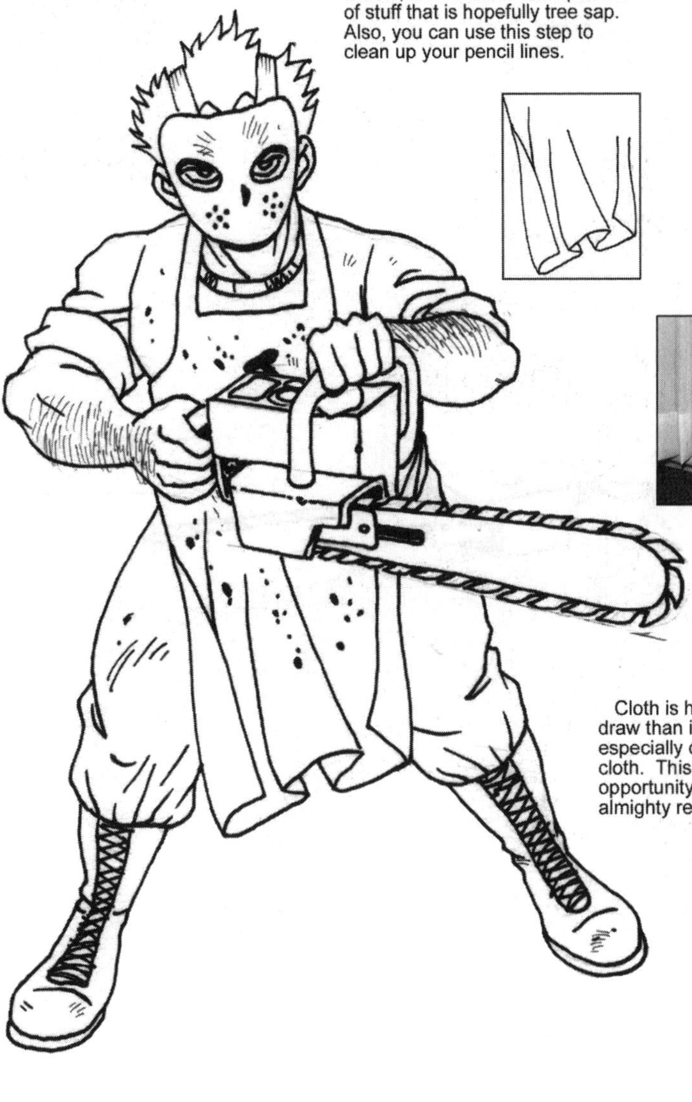

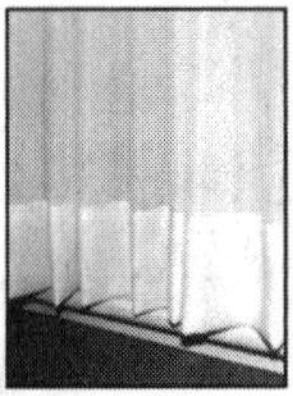

Cloth is harder to draw than it looks, especially draped cloth. This is another opportunity to use the almighty reference!

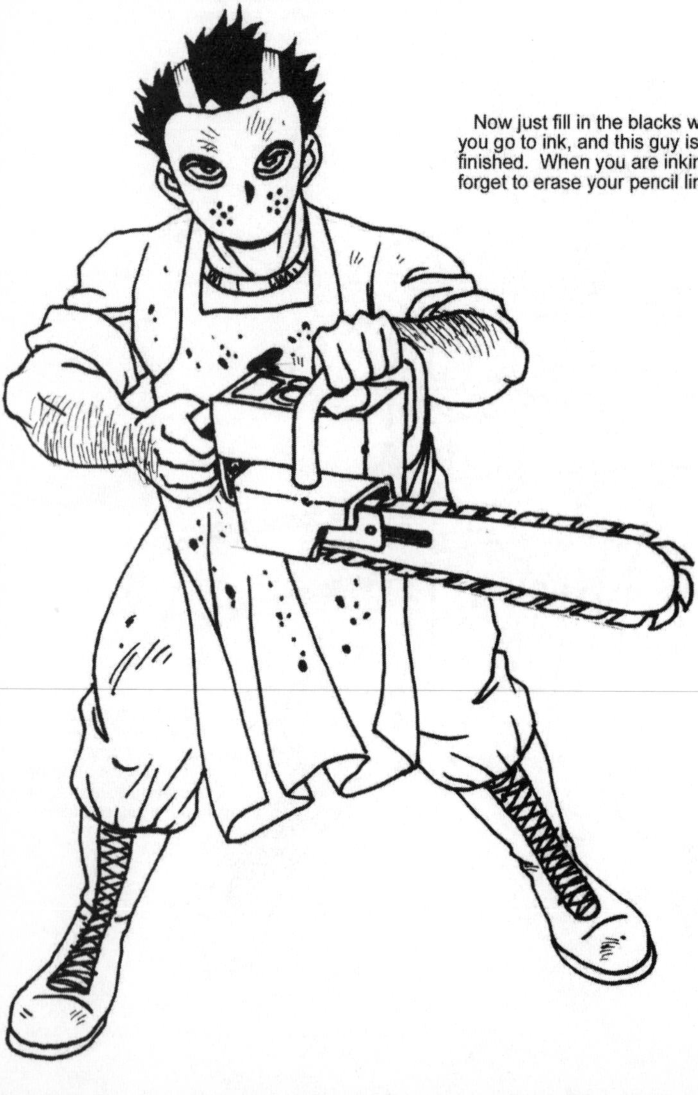

Now just fill in the blacks when you go to ink, and this guy is all finished. When you are inking, don't forget to erase your pencil lines!

PRACTICE PAGE

HOW TO DRAW MANGA

Drawing Villains

Let's take the heavy-set figure from the last section and try something different. Remember that the mass of the chest is smaller than the hips and belly.

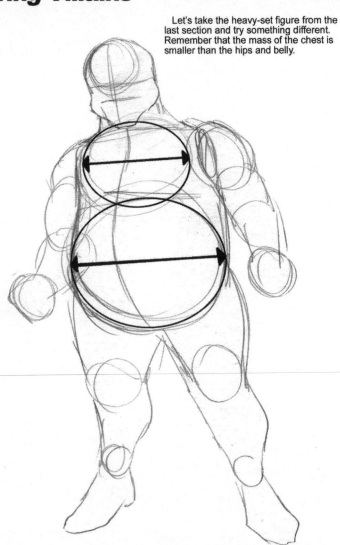

Drawing Villains

By simply adding a single element, it completely changes the direction the development of the character takes. Look at this sketch. What do you think this person could be?

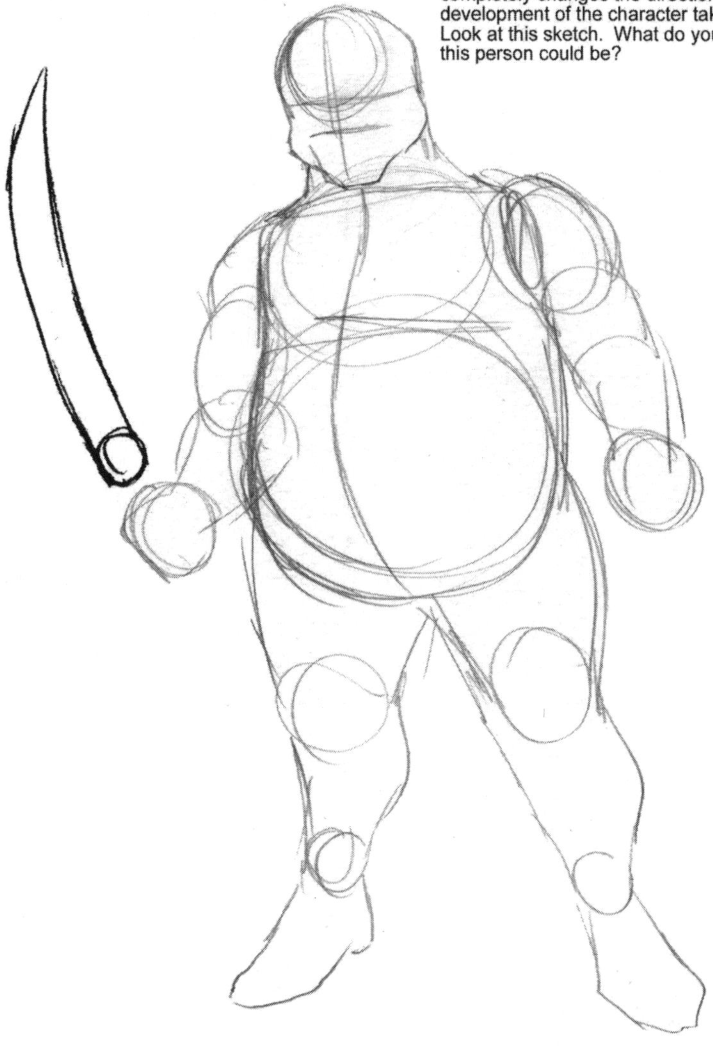

Drawing Villains

In many cases, figuring out the face can be one of the best ways to create a great character. Most artists will agree that if you can come up with a great face, the rest will fall into place. Here, the goatee, Fu Manchu mustache and missing eye already suggest a personality.

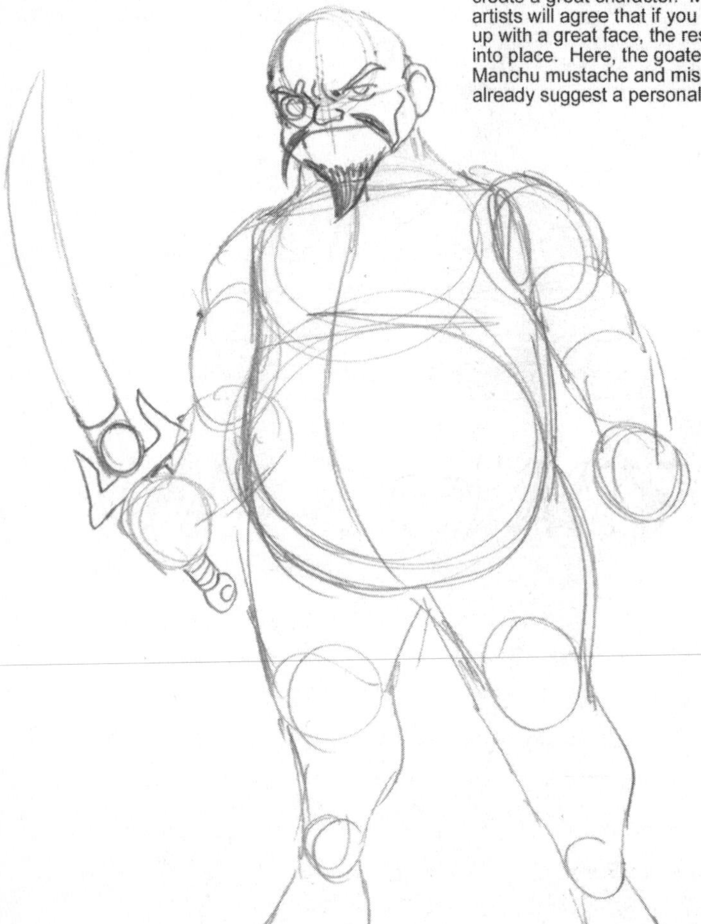

Drawing Villains

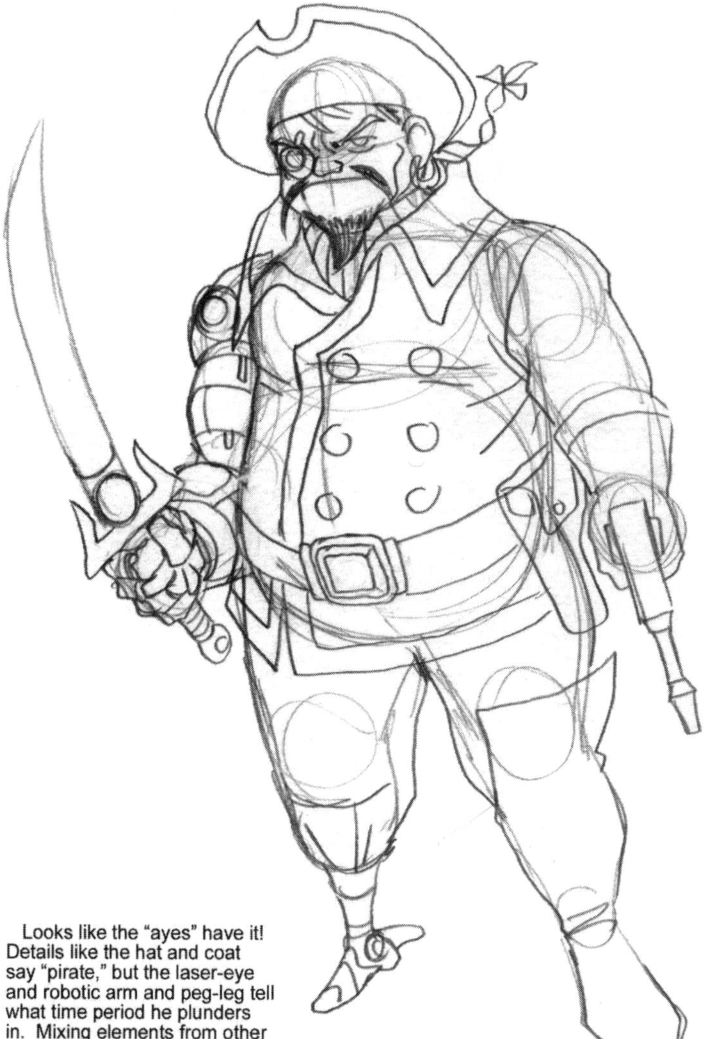

Looks like the "ayes" have it! Details like the hat and coat say "pirate," but the laser-eye and robotic arm and peg-leg tell what time period he plunders in. Mixing elements from other time periods can make for interesting combinations.

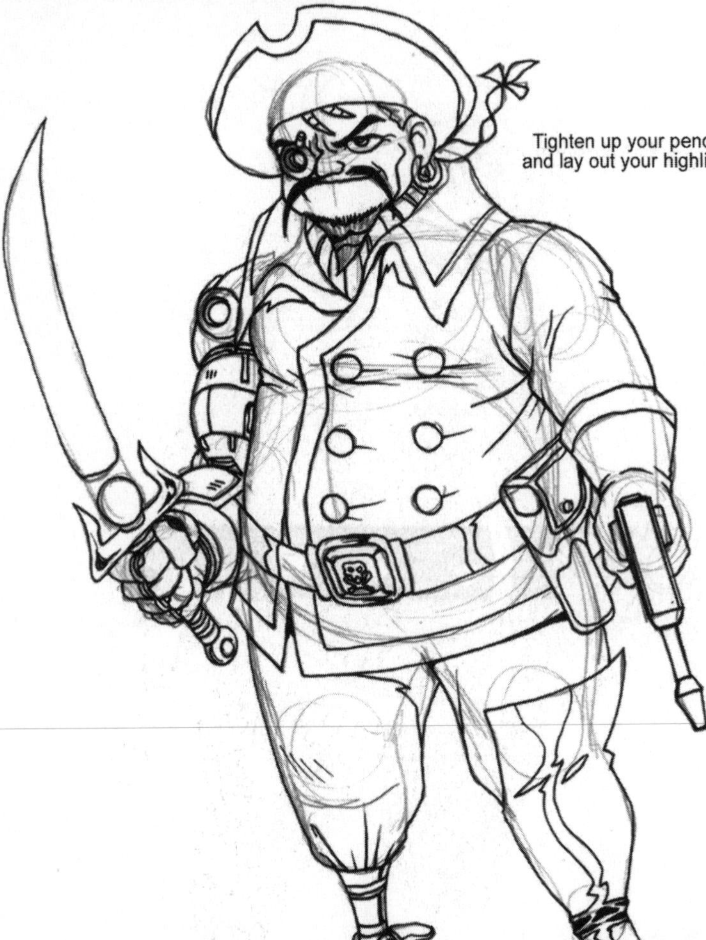

Tighten up your pencil work and lay out your highlights.

HOW TO DRAW MANGA
Drawing Villains

What kind of pirate would this
be without the obligatory parrot
on the shoulder? In this version,
though, let's make Polly a robot!

PRACTICE PAGE

HOW TO DRAW MANGA

Weapons

THE FANTASY SWORD, THE BANE OF REALISM. IN A SETTING WHERE SWORD AND SORCERY GO HAND IN HAND, THIS TYPE OF WEAPON MIGHT MAKE SENSE.

THIS IS THE KIND OF SWORD WE'RE TRYING TO GET AWAY FROM. IT'S UNBALANCED, CLUMSY AND CRUDE.

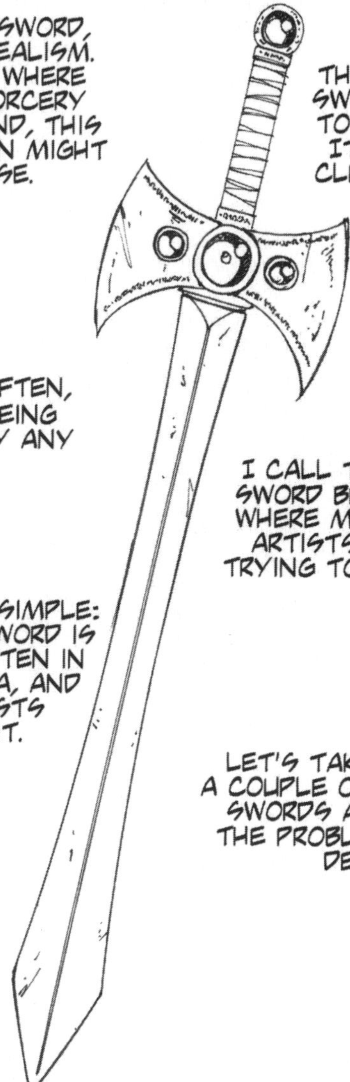

BUT ALL TOO OFTEN, I SEE THEM BEING USED IN NEARLY ANY SETTING.

I CALL THIS THE BASIC SWORD BECAUSE THIS IS WHERE MOST BEGINNING ARTISTS START WHEN TRYING TO DRAW SWORDS.

THE REASON IS SIMPLE: THIS KIND OF SWORD IS SEEN MOST OFTEN IN POPULAR MEDIA, AND SO WE ARTISTS EMULATE IT.

LET'S TAKE A LOOK AT A COUPLE OF ARCHETYPAL SWORDS AND SOME OF THE PROBLEMS IN THEIR DESIGN.

HOW TO DRAW MANGA

Weapons

HERE ARE TWO WEAPONS IN THE SERVICE OF GOOD AND EVIL, RESPECTIVELY.
NO ONE WOULD EVER USE THE SWORDS UNLESS THEY HAD NO OTHER CHOICE.
THESE ARE STRICTLY ORNAMENTS--FOR SHOW, NOT USE. THE BLADES ARE
FAR TOO LARGE AND CUMBERSOME TO BE USEFUL. LARGE HILTS COVERED WITH
SKULLS OR ENCRUSTED WITH PRECIOUS JEWELS ONLY GET IN THE WAY AND
INJURE THE PERSON USING THE SWORD. STILL, THEY LOOK KINDA COOL!

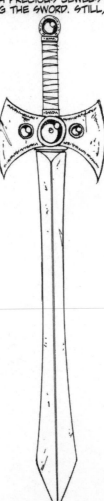

Weapons

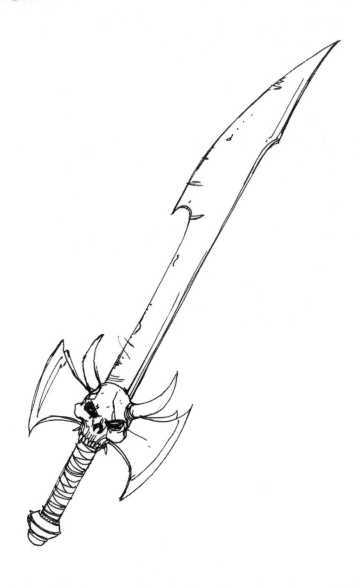

HOW TO DRAW MANGA

Weapons

NOW, THESE SWORDS MAKE A LITTLE MORE SENSE. YOU CAN DRAW
THEM FROM THEIR SHEATHS WITHOUT SEVERELY INJURING YOURSELF.
HERE FORM FOLLOWS FUNCTION, AND WE'RE NOT RIPPING OFF THE SWORD
OF OMENS. I THINK ONE OF THE MAIN PROBLEMS ARTISTS HAVE
WHEN STARTING OUT IS A LACK OF UNDERSTANDING ABOUT THEIR SUBJECT. IN
THE SAME WAY YOU CAN BENEFIT FROM A BETTER UNDERSTANDING
OF THE HUMAN BODY, YOU TRY TO FIND OUT A LITTLE ABOUT THE WEAPONS
YOU MIGHT TRY TO DEPICT.

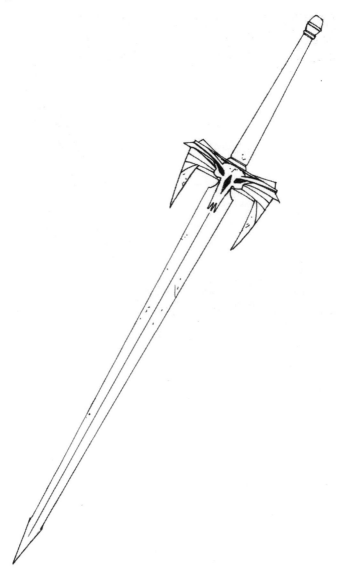

HOW TO DRAW MANGA

Weapons

LET'S TAKE A LOOK AT THE ANATOMY OF A SWORD. ALMOST ALL SWORDS SHARE A SIMILAR CONSTRUCTION AND DESIGN. I'VE LABELED THE MOST BASIC PARTS FOR MOST SWORDS.

HERE IS A DESCRIPTION OF THE BASIC PARTS AND SOME OF THE REASONING BEHIND THEM.

TANG
BLADE
CROSSGUARD
FULLER
POMMEL

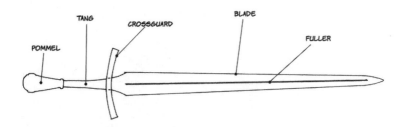

THE BLADE:
THE MOST USED PART OF THE WEAPON, MORE TIME IS PUT INTO DESIGNING THE MOST EFFECTIVE BLADE POSSIBLE. THE BLADE CAN BE DESIGNED FOR MOST ANY PURPOSE: CHOPPING, PIERCING, SLASHING, SAWING, OR HANGING ON A WALL. THEY ARE ALSO MADE TO FIT INTO CERTAIN STYLES OF FIGHTING.

THE FULLER:
KNOWN MORE OFTEN AS THE BLOODGROOVE, THE FULLER IS A WEDGE-SHAPED GROOVE THAT FOLLOWS THE LENGTH OF THE SWORD. WHEN THE OPPONENT IS STABBED WITH THE SWORD, A VACUUM MAY CLOSE AROUND THE BLADE, MAKING IT NEARLY IMPOSSIBLE TO PULL THE WEAPON OUT AGAIN.
THE FULLER CHANNELS BLOOD FROM THE WOUND, MAKING IT EASIER TO WITHDRAW THE SWORD.

THE TANG:
THE TANG IS THE PART OF THE SWORD THAT CONTINUES DOWN PAST THE HILT AND INTO THE HANDLE. SOME TANGS CONTINUE AS ONE PIECE TO BECOME THE POMMEL.

Weapons

THE HILT OR CROSSGUARD:

MEANT TO HELP BLOCK THE BLOW FROM A SWORD. IT ALSO PROTECTS THE HANDS FROM BEING INJURED IN BATTLE. DEPENDING ON THE DESIGN, IT CAN ALSO BE USED TO TRAP AN OPPONENT'S SWORD OR TO HELP DISARM THE OPPONENT.

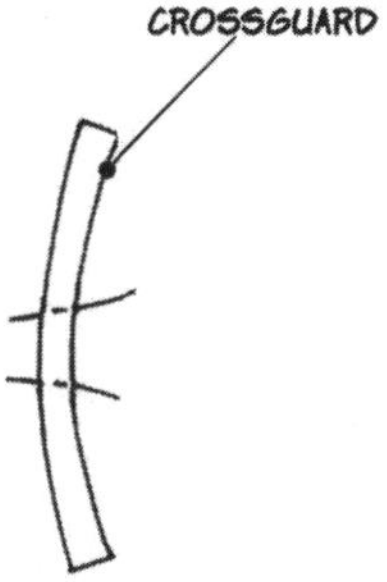
CROSSGUARD

THE HANDLE AND GRIP:

THE HANDLE IS TYPICALLY MADE OF WOOD, THOUGH HORN AND OTHER MATERIALS ARE USED. THE HANDLE SURROUNDS THE TANG AND MAY BE FASTENED BY BOLTS OR CORD. THE GRIP IS USUALLY LEATHER OR CORD.

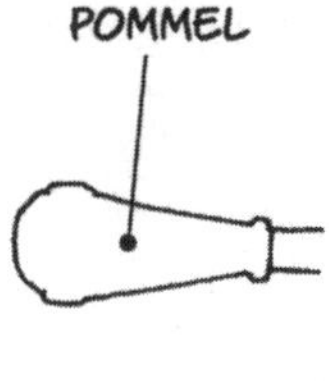
POMMEL

THE POMMEL:

THE POMMEL IS NOT JUST THERE TO REST YOUR HAND ON, IT'S MEANT TO DELIVER DAMAGE. WHEN DRAWING THE SWORD, IT CAN BE USED TO STRIKE THE HEAD AND CHEST OF THE OPPONENT. IN BATTLE, IT TAKES AWAY THE ENEMY'S ABILITY TO USE A WEAPON BY SHATTERING BONES AND DAMAGING MUSCLE TISSUE IN THE HANDS, ARM AND SHOULDER.

HERE ARE THE BASIC STEPS FOR DRAWING A STANDARD SWORD.

NOW LET'S TAKE A LOOK AT SOME DIFFERENT TYPES OF SWORDS AND SOME OF THE REASONS BEHIND THEIR DESIGN.

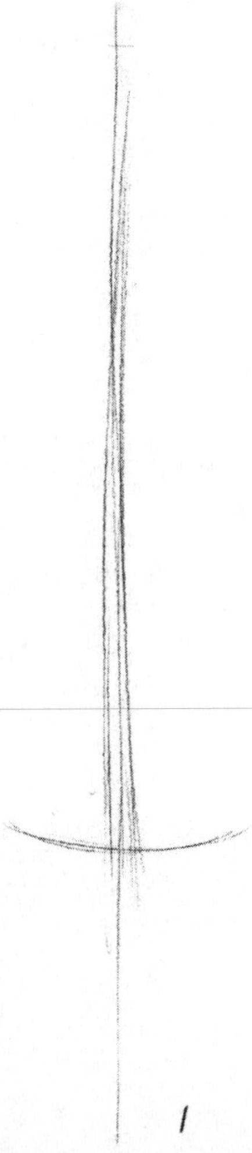
1

Weapons

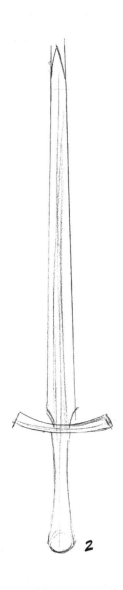

2

PRACTICE PAGE

Weapons

ALSO KNOWN AS "THE NINJA SWORD", THE KATANA IS MADE FOR SMOOTH, FLUID MOVEMENTS PRIMARILY A SLASHING WEAPON, WITH IT, AN EXPERT COULD CLEAVE AN ADULT MALE IN HALF WITH ONE BLOW. MANY OF THESE SWORDS ARE CONSIDERED WORKS OF ART. HERE I SHOW WHAT THE TANG OF THE BLADE LOOKS LIKE.

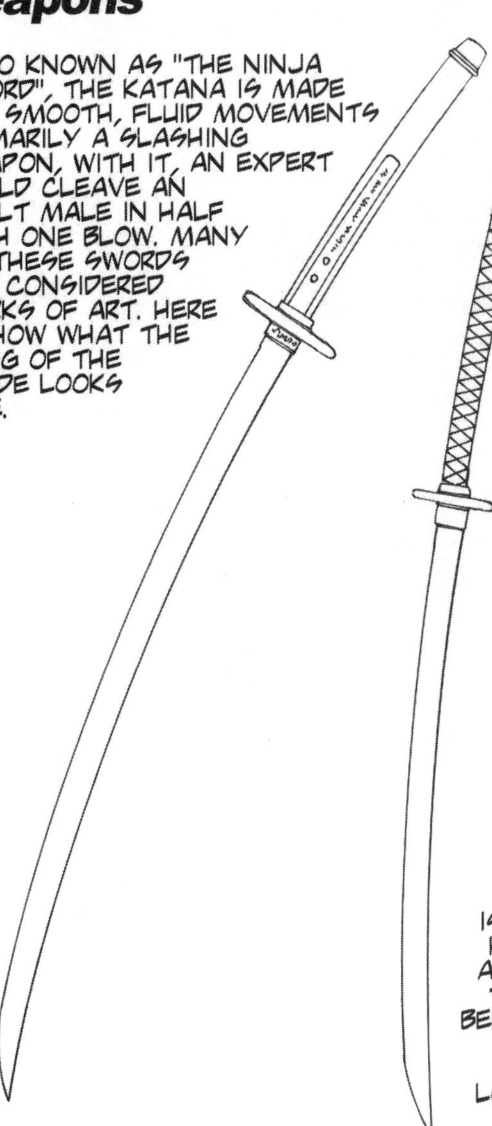

THE BLADE OF THIS NAGINATA IS SIMILAR TO THE KATANA, THOUGH A LITTLE SHORTER. THE HANDLE HAS BEEN EXTENDED INTO A POLEARM FOR LEVERAGE AND LONGER REACH FOR THE WEAPON.

Weapons

LIGHT AND FLEXIBLE, THE RAPIER IS MADE TO STAB VITAL ORGANS WITH PRECISION. WITH PROPER SKILL, A SWORDSMAN CAN DEFEAT AN ARMOURED OPPONENT BY EXPLOITING WEAK SPOTS. SOME OF THESE SWORDS ARE SO WELL MADE THAT THEY CAN EVEN PIERCE THE ARMOUR ITSELF.

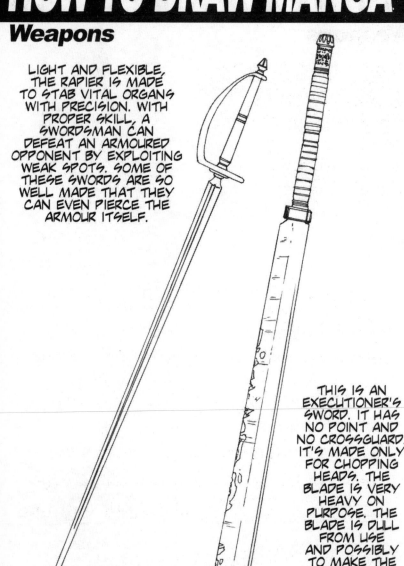

THIS IS AN EXECUTIONER'S SWORD. IT HAS NO POINT AND NO CROSSGUARD. IT'S MADE ONLY FOR CHOPPING HEADS. THE BLADE IS VERY HEAVY ON PURPOSE. THE BLADE IS DULL FROM USE AND POSSIBLY TO MAKE THE BEHEADING TAKE LONGER.

Weapons

LONG AND HEAVY, THE BASTARD SWORD IS MADE FOR SMASHING DOWN AN OPPONENT. WHILE EFFECTIVE, THESE SWORDS COULD ONLY BE USED BY THE MANLIEST OF MEN. THE SPIKES ON THE BLADE CAN BE USED CRACK AN ENEMY HELMET. THIS IS THE DOUBLE-HANDED VERSION, ONE OF MY FAVORITE SWORDS. IF YOU WANT TO SEE THIS SWORD IN USE, RENT A COPY OF "BRAVEHEART."

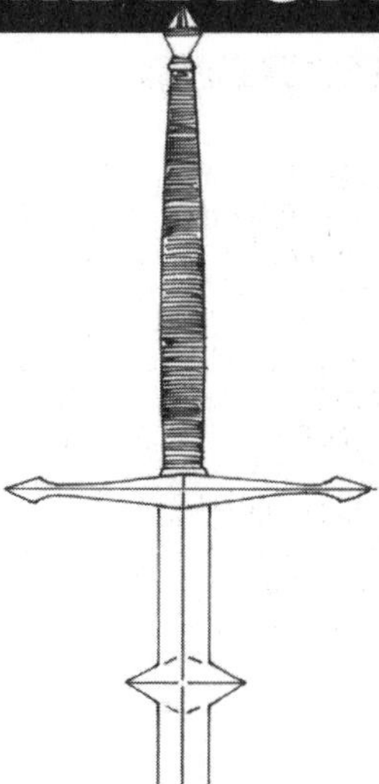

HERE ARE SOME OF THE SWORDS I'VE DESIGNED FROM LOOKING AT DIFFERENT SWORDS.

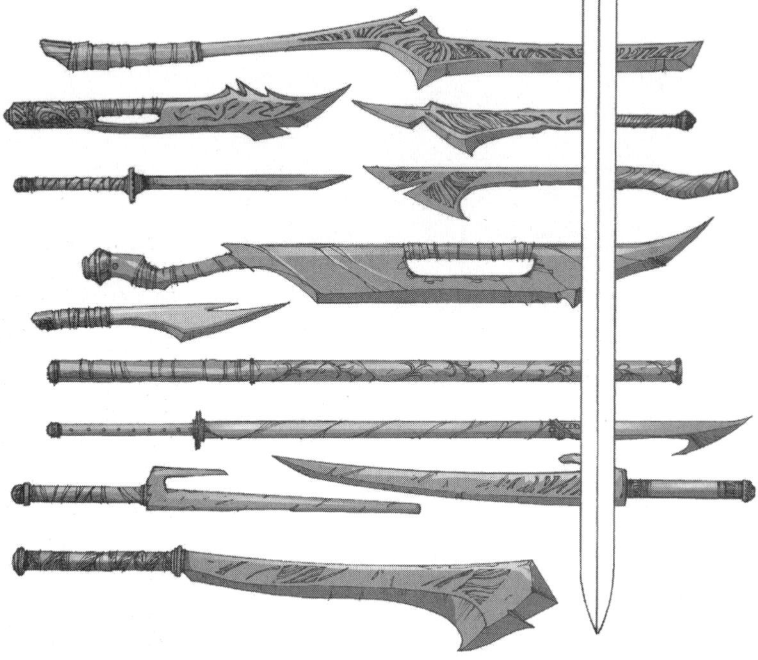

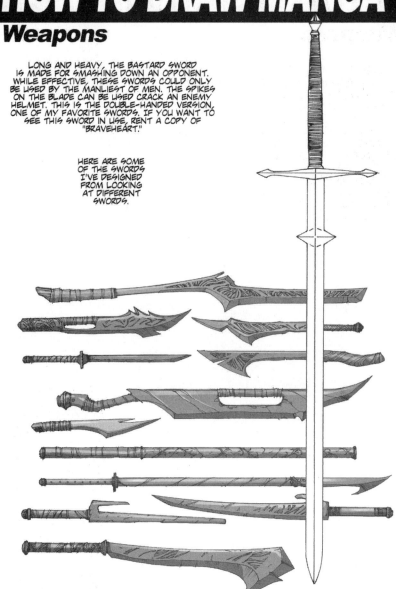

Weapons

To make your guns realistic-looking, you must draw as much as possible from references. Futuristic guns are also based on present-day weapons. The gun on the bottom row is based on the one above it—with slight modifications. Slightly changing certain features while retaining overall appearance is the key to making futuristic guns look real.

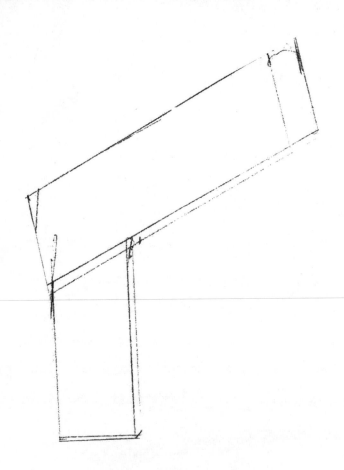

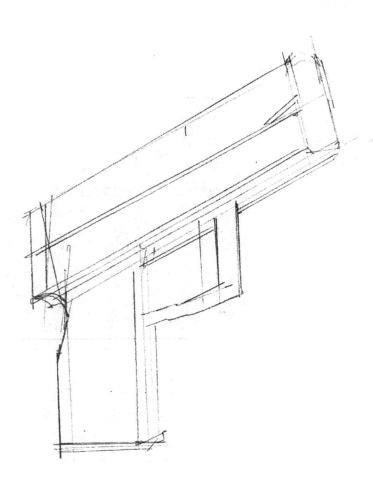

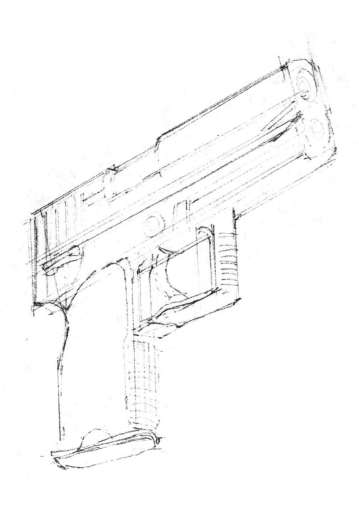

HOW TO DRAW MANGA

Weapons

PRACTICE PAGE

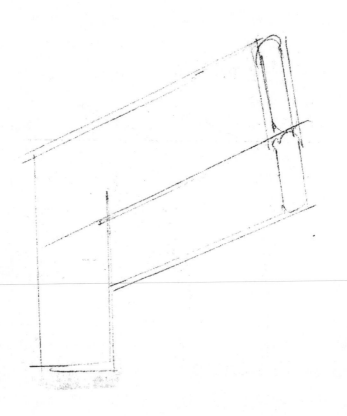

HOW TO DRAW MANGA

Weapons

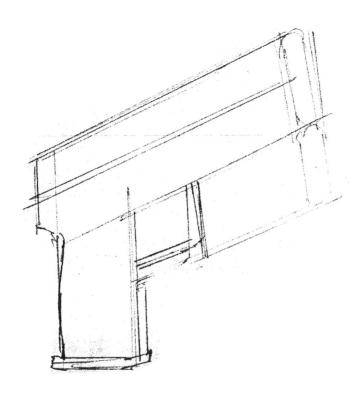

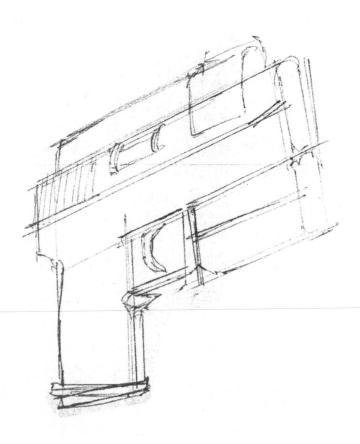

HOW TO DRAW MANGA

Weapons

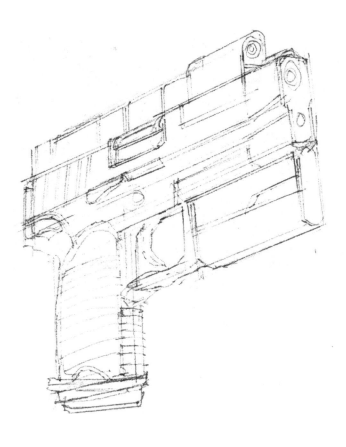

HOW TO DRAW MANGA
Weapons

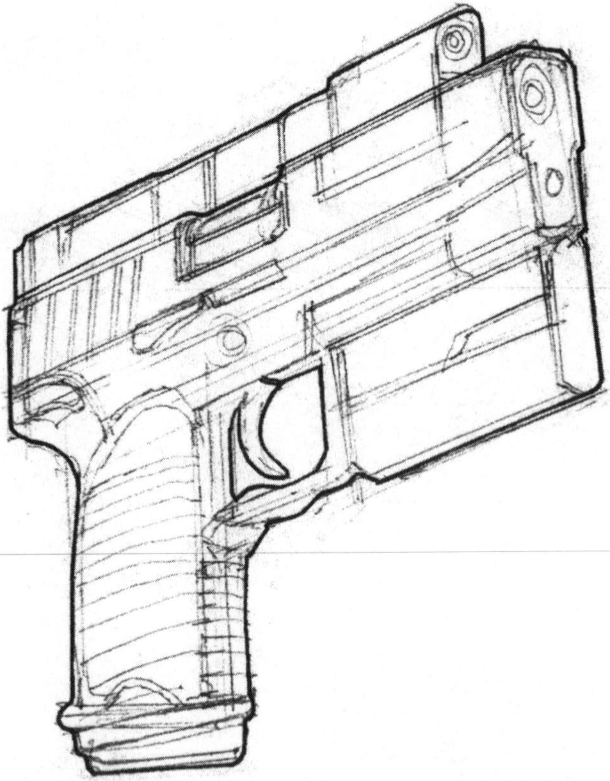

HOW TO DRAW MANGA

Weapons

HOW TO DRAW MANGA

Weapons

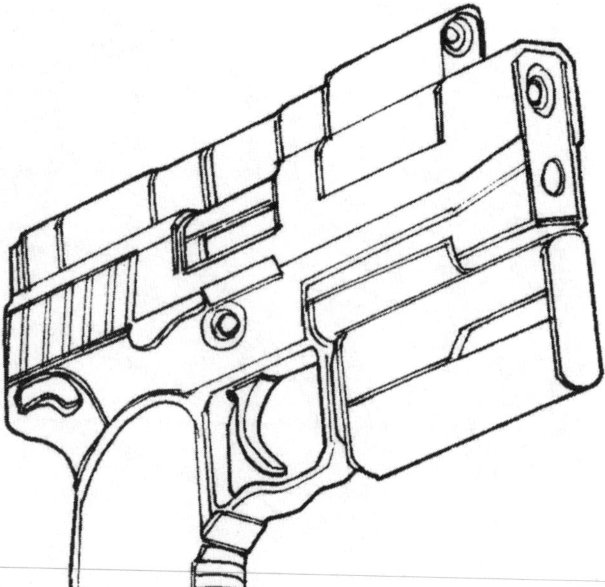

PRACTICE PAGE

Weapons

The M16 Rifle is the standard weapon of choice of most military organizations in the world today. It is the symbol of Western might.

Here, we start off with the simplest of shapes--a box.

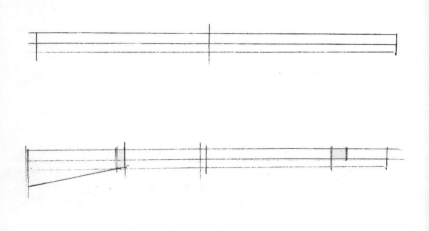

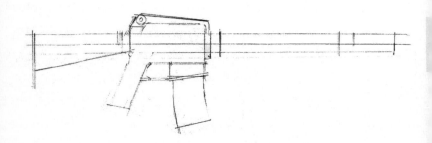

HOW TO DRAW MANGA

Weapons

Knowing how to draw guns from real life will help you draw
realistic futuristic weapons later on. As with basic human anatomy,
having a good working knowledge of how things work
is the key to success.

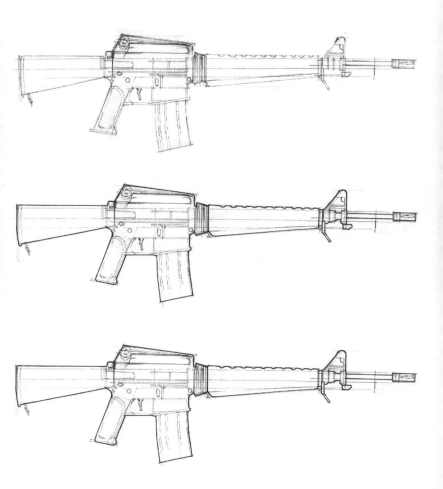

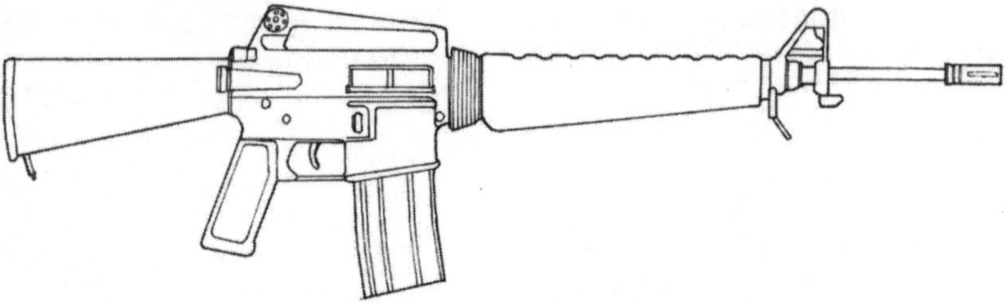

Adding a few trinkets makes this regular weapon look high tech while remaining very much believable.
This design is based on something I once saw in a movie: a regular M16 with a shotgun instead of the grenade launcher.
More and more equipment can be added to this.
The idea is to keep the basic familiar shape intact.

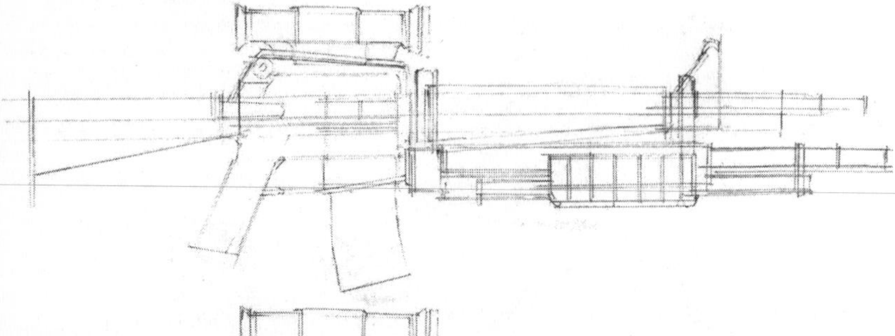

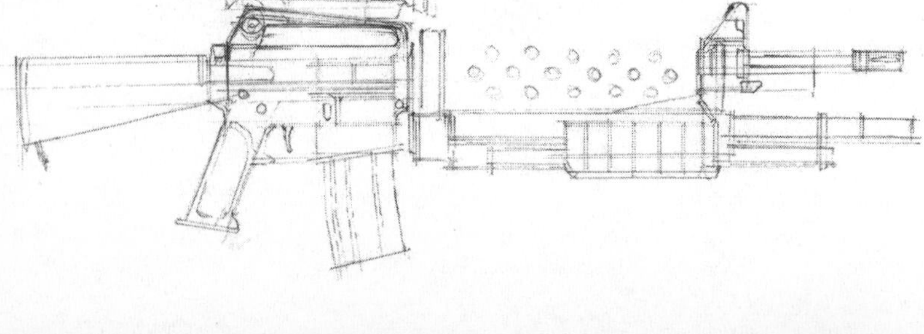

Weapons

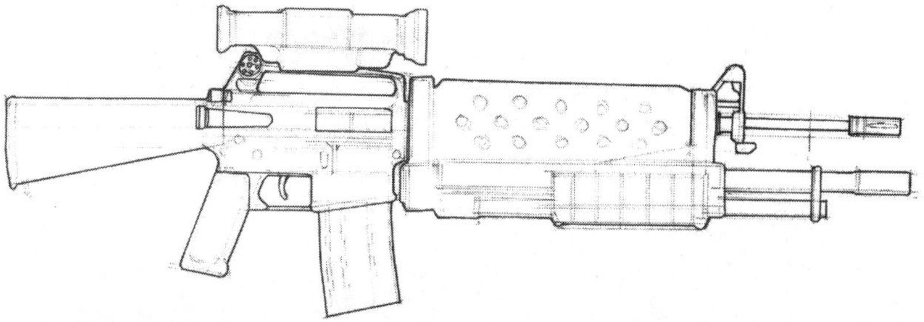

Authors are encouraged to write about what they know. There is a reason for this. Writing about things you know firsthand makes your work more authentic. Drawing comics is like writing. You have to know what you are drawing.

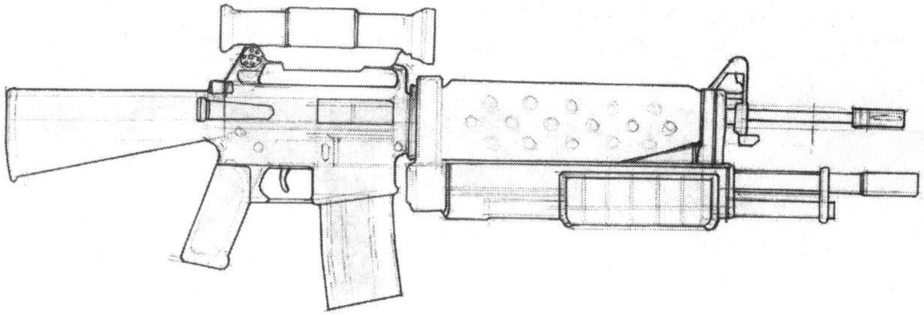

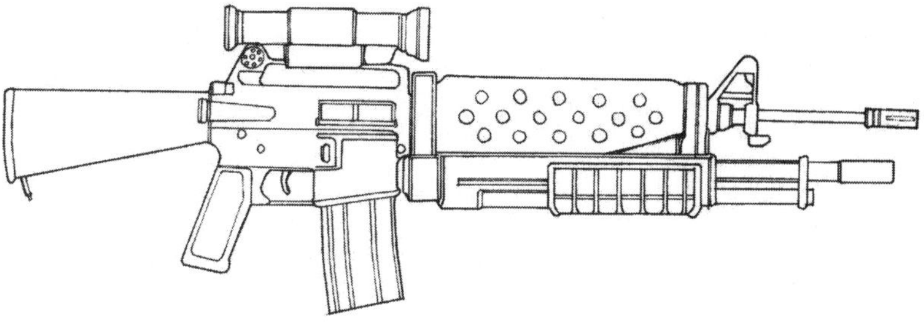

PRACTICE PAGE

Weapons

In the end, there is still more and more to learn. This is what makes art so exciting. There is always a new horizon waiting to be explored. Just as you think you have mastered one thing, there is always another to be learned. Or perhaps we think we know all there is about one thing, only to find out we still have a long way to go. It takes a lifetime to master it all.

HOW TO DRAW MANGA

Human Monsters

This werewolf does a great job of tying the human and animal forms together. There is very little doubt that this creature is a wolf, and at the same time, you can look at it and clearly see that at one point it was a human and will probably take that form again soon.

HOW TO DRAW MANGA
Human Monsters

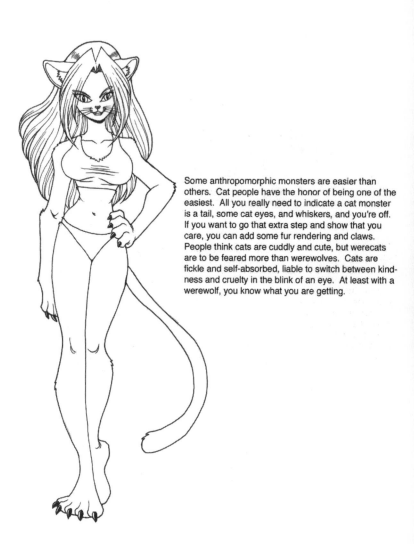

Some anthropomorphic monsters are easier than others. Cat people have the honor of being one of the easiest. All you really need to indicate a cat monster is a tail, some cat eyes, and whiskers, and you're off. If you want to go that extra step and show that you care, you can add some fur rendering and claws. People think cats are cuddly and cute, but werecats are to be feared more than werewolves. Cats are fickle and self-absorbed, liable to switch between kindness and cruelty in the blink of an eye. At least with a werewolf, you know what you are getting.

Cat pupils are slitted, unlike round human pupils.

Cats are able to retract their claws back into their paws.

Some people hypothesize that every creature has the genetic potential of every other creature locked away in its body. With a little genetic reforming, you might look like this. A fish/human hybrid will have a whole different set of problems and personality issues from the cat and wolf people. First, does a fishman need water every time he transforms? Can he breath air? The scary thing about a werefish is that his species has a lot to be upset about: A "small" amount of pollution in his ocean affects the delicate balance under the waves.

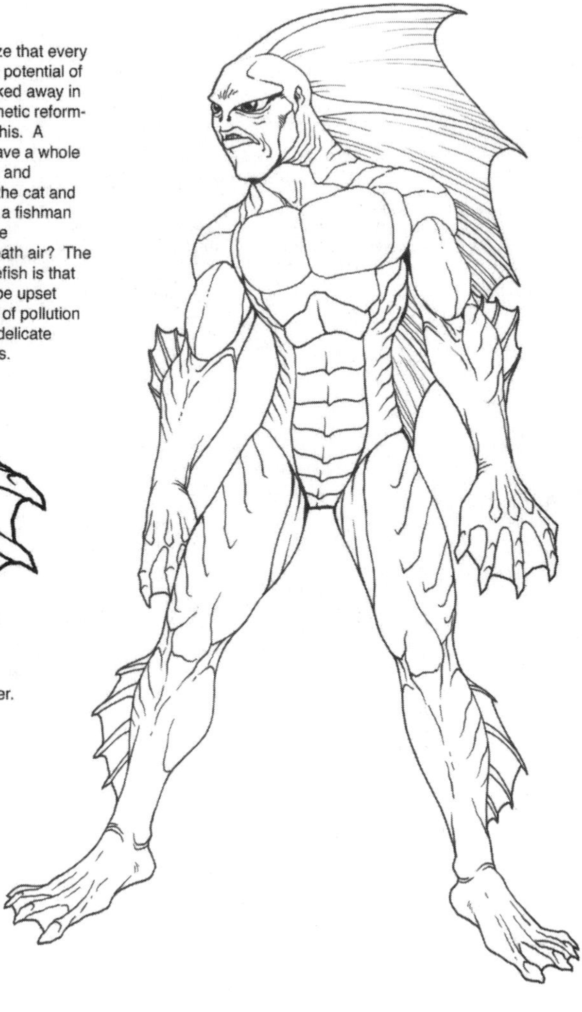

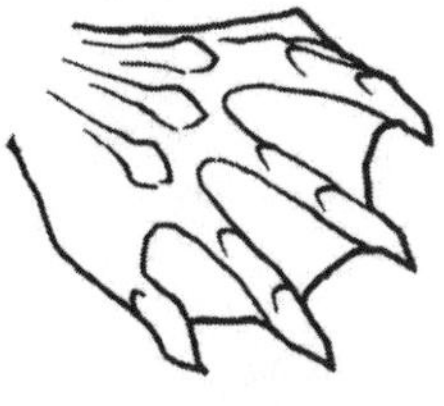

Webbed fingers help fishmen to move easily and quickly through water.

HOW TO DRAW MANGA
Human Monsters

A lot of transforming monsters fit very easily into stories about the environment. They can be seen as noble monsters defending the environment, but sometimes people transform themselves through science for selfish reasons. This insectman injected himself with an experimental formula that he hoped would allow him to make use of some of the positive aspects of insect life. Instead he ended up like this. He is understandably upset, and his new-found strength makes him a large threat.

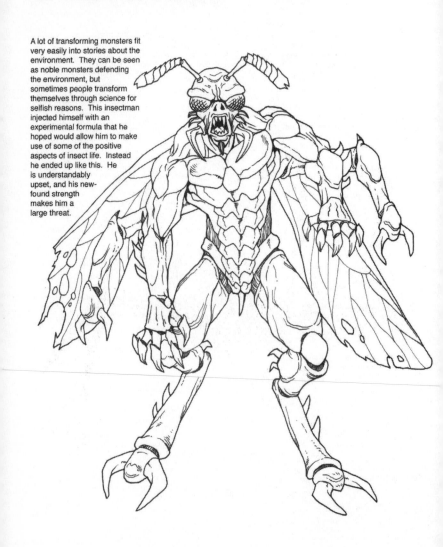

HOW TO DRAW MANGA
Human Monsters

Some transforming monsters developed the ability to transform into human form as a way to hunt. This Black Widow Monster uses her human form to lure men to her lair, where she kills them and keeps them on wrap for later snacking. Arachnophobia is very common, and a good storyteller will exploit the fears of his readers to chill and thrill them.

PRACTICE PAGE

HOW TO DRAW MANGA

Giant Monsters

Kaiju, or giant monsters, have their roots in the advent of the atomic age. Following the second World War, the cultural apprehension of the Japanese people concerning what atomic fallout might do to the world and the threat of the Cold War were expressed in films showcasing creatures that had often been created by radioactivity. The prevalence of radiation paranoia throughout the world, along with the high level of entertainment the films provided, made Giant Monster movies a global success, and their popularity continues to this day.

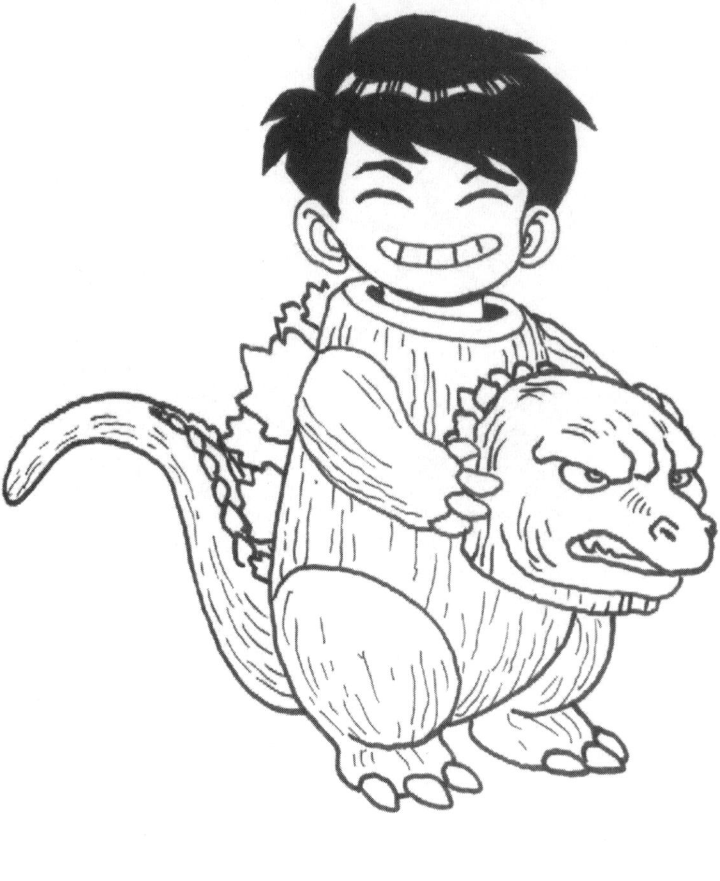

HOW TO DRAW MANGA

Giant Monsters

Just as Giant Monsters can be literally anything, you can tell a dizzying array of stories centered around a giant monster. Anything from a story of catastrophe to a romance can be effectively told in this sub-genre of monster movie. The freedom of Giant Monster stories is one of the things that makes them so much fun.

HOW TO DRAW MANGA

Giant Monsters

When creating a Giant Monster, there are four basic types to choose from: Quadrupedal, Arthropoid, Shapeless, or Bipedal.

The Quadruped body type walks on four legs. These creatures will move in the same way as regular four-legged animals. Four legs give them a great deal of stability, but it usually means that they are shorter in height. To make up for this, they sometimes rear up on their hind legs to attack.

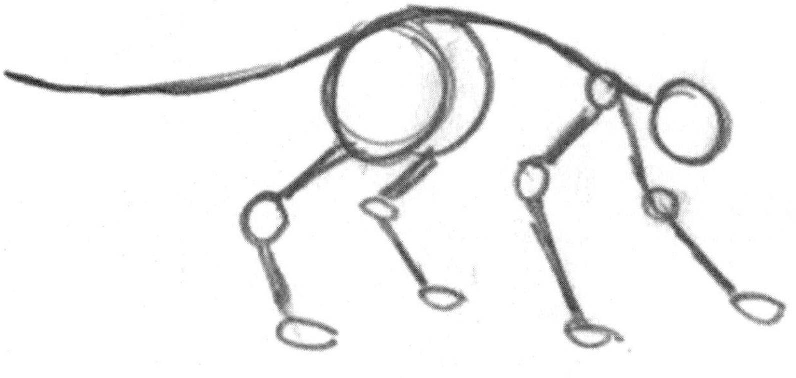

Giant Monsters

Quadruped monsters are
particularly suited to stories in
which you desire for your
monster to convey a bestial
character. It is harder to relate
to a creature on four legs than
on two. There is a wealth of
reference to draw from, as the
number of four-legged species
on Earth numbers in the
thousands.

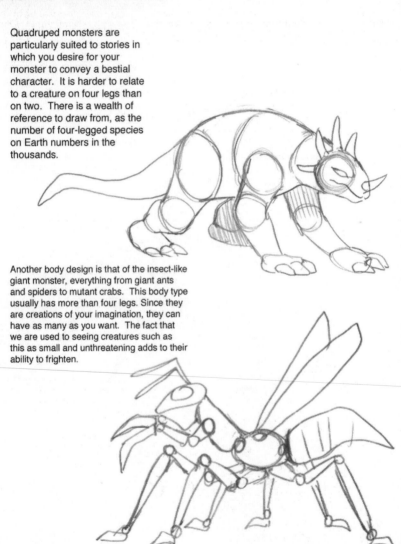

Another body design is that of the insect-like
giant monster, everything from giant ants
and spiders to mutant crabs. This body type
usually has more than four legs. Since they
are creations of your imagination, they can
have as many as you want. The fact that
we are used to seeing creatures such as
this as small and unthreatening adds to their
ability to frighten.

HOW TO DRAW MANGA

Giant Monsters

There are a number of creatures that do not really have a specific category. Sometimes they have no bones, like a squid, octopus, or slime. Other monsters have shapes that they alter regularly. A silicon monster made completely of sand that doesn't stay in one shape for very long or a Giant Monster made entirely of light would be examples of this. Finally, some body shapes, like a snake's, are unique and highly recognizable but not really deserving of their own specification.

Giant Squid are one of the few Giant Monsters that really exist. This can make stories centering on them seem more realistic. Giant sea monsters have a long tradition in most cultures of the world that border on water, so there is a wealth of information to choose from. Anything from sea serpents to man-eating oysters works as a story concept.

Don't feel that a creature's natural environment limits its story potential. Nothing shakes up a reader like unexpected behavior. I highly urge you to take your inspiration, in this case a squid, out of its natural environment and experiment.

In this image, a squid is on land in front of a schoolhouse. This does not agree with what conventional knowledge says is true of squid, so one has to wonder in what other ways this squid is unique.

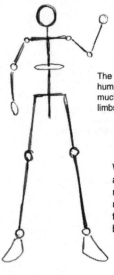

The final and most common type of Giant Monster is the bipedal or humanoid body type. These monsters walk on two legs and move in much the same way as humans. This means that they often have front limbs to attack with as well as a wide range of motion for the head.

When designing a bipedal monster, you can usually start with the basic human body design.

Sometimes a bipedal monster will be significantly different in structure from a human, like this monster based on an avian design.

HOW TO DRAW MANGA

Giant Monsters

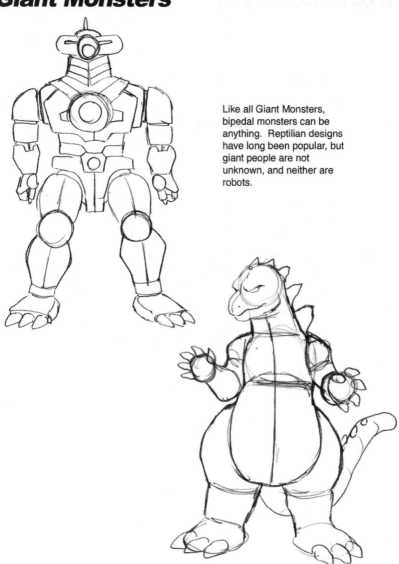

Like all Giant Monsters, bipedal monsters can be anything. Reptilian designs have long been popular, but giant people are not unknown, and neither are robots.

HOW TO DRAW MANGA

Giant Monsters

Step 1.

When drawing a bipedal Giant Monster, make sure that its shape is balanced. Ask yourself, "Would this creature be able to support its own weight in real life, and would it be able to stand on two legs? Where would its arms be? Would they be attached to its shoulders or somewhere else on its chest?"

Let's see how a Giant Monster develops step by step. We have decided to draw a very classic design: the Thunder Lizard, a cross between a Tyrannosaurus Rex and a regular lizard. Something about a cold-blooded monster just appeals to me. They are both terrestrial, in that we have encounters with them regularly, and alien, in that they are cold-blooded and totally different from us biologically.

Giant Monsters

Step 2.

After establishing the basic shape of our
Giant Monster, we can begin to add some
details. It is covered with overlapping bone
plates for protection, a design element
shared with the armadillo. Bony spines
along its back, arms, and head give it a more
menacing appearance.

From Step 1 to Step 2, there are a wide range of design choices that can be made. We could
have instead chosen to make our Giant Monster sleek and smooth or even hairy. Try photo-
copying the previous page and experimenting with different ways of developing the basic
shape we laid out.

HOW TO DRAW MANGA

Giant Monsters

Step 3.

A little rendering develops the different textures of the monster. It is now looking very threatening. There is a clear difference between the plating and the unprotected skin, shown by the addition of the wrinkles in the skin. This image is now ready to be inked.

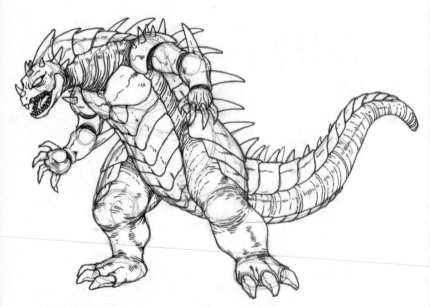

Variety keeps your monster from looking dull. The different types of plating are the key in this drawing, from the rounded shoulder guard to the breast plate and horned head plate.

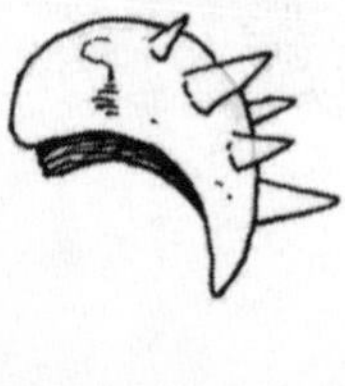

HOW TO DRAW MANGA

Giant Monsters

Step 4.

After inking your Giant Monster, erase your pencil lines, and you have a gargantuan terror ready to destroy a city, do battle with another mutation of nature, or just scare the local wildlife.

This is just one example, and a fairly traditional one at that, of a Giant Monster. When creating your own, you can draw from the classics or do something totally different. The beauty of monsters is that the newer and more creative, the more interesting and scary they can be.

PRACTICE PAGE

Giant Monsters

Bipedal monsters can take a great number of shapes. It is very important that you do not become caught up in the idea of making them look human simply because they have two legs. They can have multiple heads, tentacles instead of arms, or wings. It is even okay if they lack certain things that would be expected. A giant bipedal monster without a head would be pretty shocking.

A fight between bipedal monsters is easy to construct and follow visually, since we are used to looking at two upright figures interact.

HOW TO DRAW MANGA

Giant Monsters

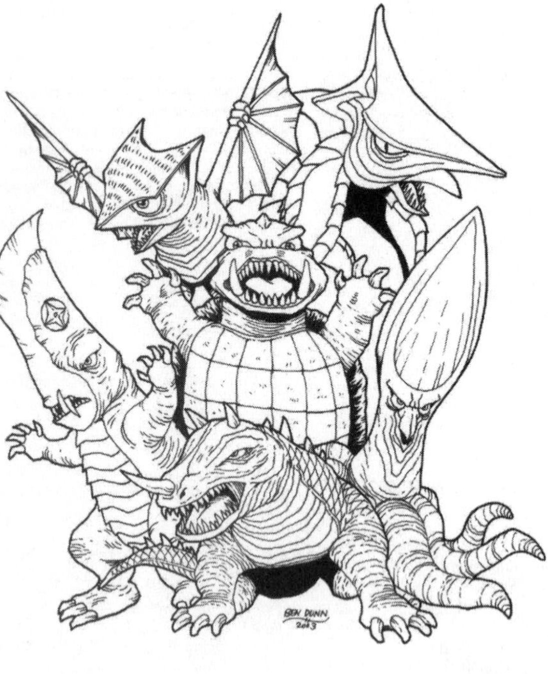

Sniff....Giant Monsters really are beautiful. It just tugs on your heart strings...as you run in terror, of course. Never forget the running and the terror and the screaming.

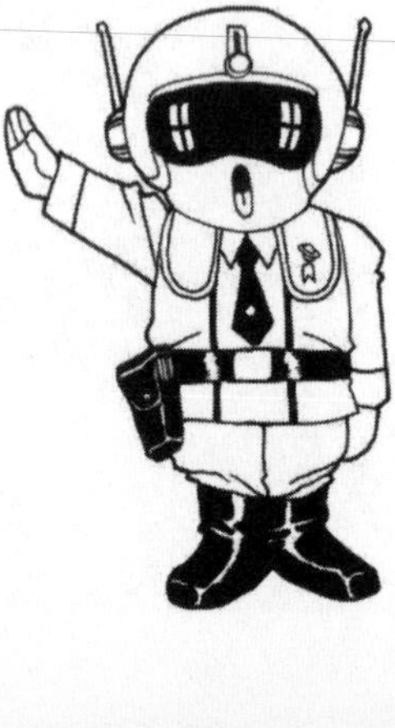

But wait...what's this? There's more? What could be better than a Giant Monster in its element? How about all the other variations on this theme? Let's take a look!

Giant Monsters

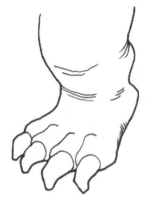

A nice, clawed stomper is great, but there are so many other kinds of feet out there to choose from, some of them slightly different, others unique to the extreme.

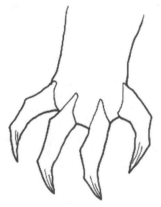

A modified anteater claw! If it's good for dissecting an anthill, why wouldn't it be good for dissecting a building?

A wing-mounted claw...might not be as effective as a wing-mounted heat-seeking missile, but when you're invincible and 100 feet tall, you're not complaining.

HOW TO DRAW MANGA

Giant Monsters

I'm gonna get you! Okay, maybe I won't, but human hands are pretty good at squashing bugs. Think how much better they would work if they had palms the size of a truck.

When you walk on lava, your feet may look a bit different. No one is complaining as long as they remain uncharred.

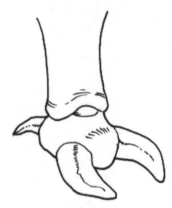

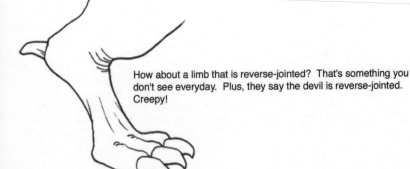

How about a limb that is reverse-jointed? That's something you don't see everyday. Plus, they say the devil is reverse-jointed. Creepy!

HOW TO DRAW MANGA

Giant Monsters

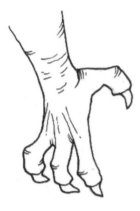

I have never really appreciated my pinkies, so this design appeals to me, although nail-trimming is probably a real problem.

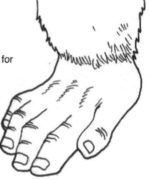

How's this look to you, monkey fans? Great for cradling the damsel of your banana-filled dreams.

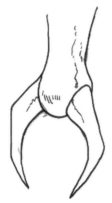

A nice pointy pincer for...pointing and pincing, I guess.

Giant Monsters

Nothing like a trio of rending claws to make a good impression—well, some kind of impression, at least.

A bird's wings look fairly normal, but not when they are attached to a shambling, reptilian bog monster. Although you can stuff a pillow pretty fast with 8-foot feathers.

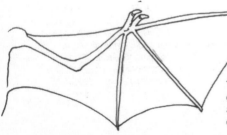

These bat-like wings can carry a great deal more weight than you would imagine and create gale-force winds as an offensive attack.

Giant Monsters

Ahh...the beauty of a butterfly's wing, so colorful, so soft, almost hypnotic. All the better for a Giant Monster who wants to appear unthreatening up until he eats your town hall.

Insect wings beat at a very rapid rate, sometimes moving so fast that they blur into invisibility. They also catch light and filter it into dazzling prismatic displays.

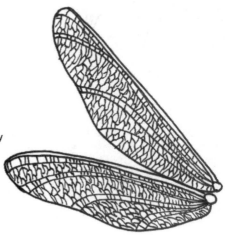

Tentacles! Many is the time I have wished for a few tentacles to help me out during the day. Some creatures have all the luck. They are extremely versatile, and just about any Giant Monster can benefit from a few.

Giant Monsters

Skin–you got it, I got it, and so do most Giant monsters. Of course, theirs might not be as soft and fragile as ours. They probably have cold-resistant, fireproof, radioactive super skin.

A big concern of the Giant Monster youth of today is skin blemishes, but sometimes the warty look is just something you have to accept.

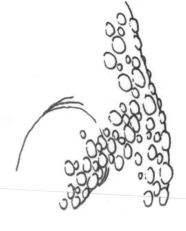

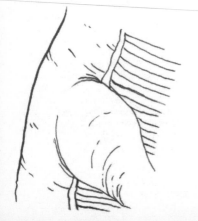

While humans just have one major skin type, Giant Monsters can often have two or three or ten.

Giant Monsters

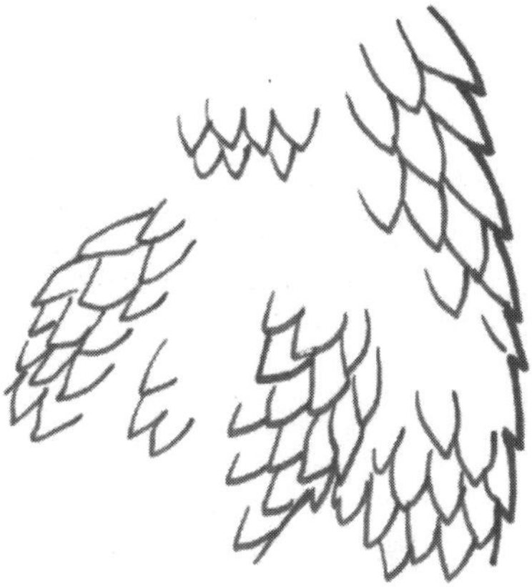

Scales are great for protection. The way they overlap means that every inch of your body is covered, plus you dry out a lot faster than those Giant Monsters with fur.

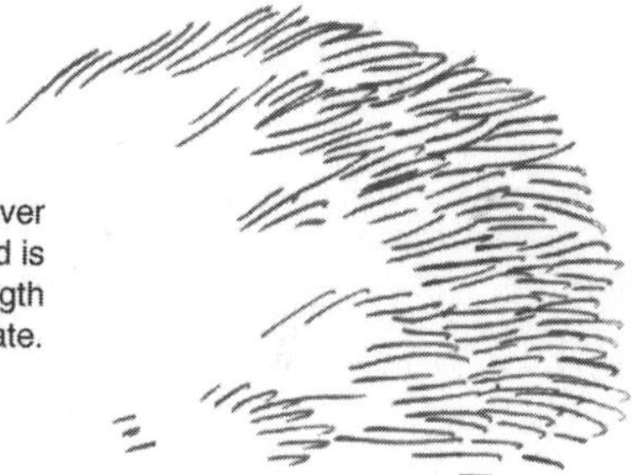

Fur is comprised of lots of short hairs that cover most of your body. It can be any color and is very functional. Usually, fur grows at a length suited to a creature's current climate.

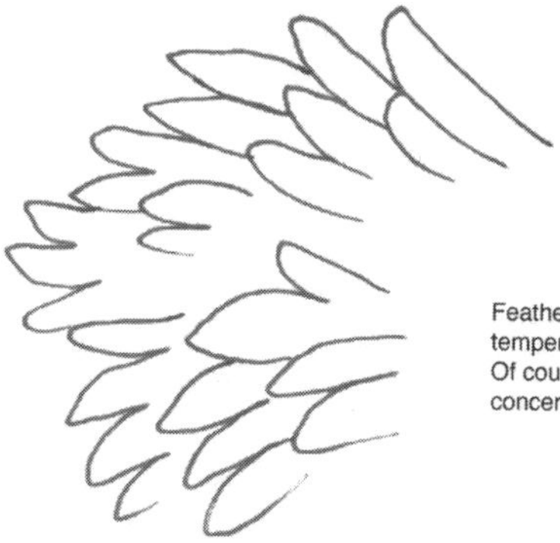

Feathers can be a blessing and a curse. They provide great temperature control, but sometimes you look a little like a sissy. Of course, once you peck someone's head off, that really isn't a concern anymore.

Giant Monsters

When a Giant Monster is hairy, it is covered all over with long hair. This allows a Giant Monster to develop a suitably repugnant odor if it stays away from water long enough, and smaller creatures can make their home in its hair. Everyone wins!

Fish scales are great because they are almost always accompanied by a slimy body coating, which comes in real handy when grappling with other Giant Monsters.

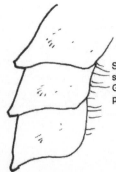

Sectional armor can be formed by bone plates, extra-tough leathery skin, oversized scales, or even mineral deposits that have grown on a Giant Monster over the eons. As far as defense goes, this may be the peak, as it provides both maneuverability and protection.

HOW TO DRAW MANGA

Giant Monsters

Sometimes a Giant Monster will wear armor or be built with metal skin or maybe even grow it. A shiny metal exterior requires constant attention in the form of polishing or dips in a boiling natural spring. A good heat-scouring in a lava pit can also do the trick.

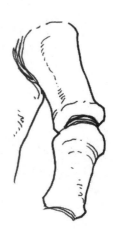

Chitin plating is common among insect monsters. It acts both to contain an insect's internal organs and to protect it from aggression. Chitin has been known to have a glossy and shiny appearance which can be quite breathtaking.

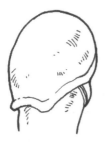

A dull metal exterior can sometimes be the clever deception of a monster trying to appear old and lazy.

Giant Monsters

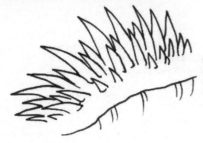

Spiny, porcupine-like skin can be a great defense, and when you can shoot your spines at high speeds, it can also be a great offensive weapon. Nothing says "Stay away" like a four-foot spike of hair.

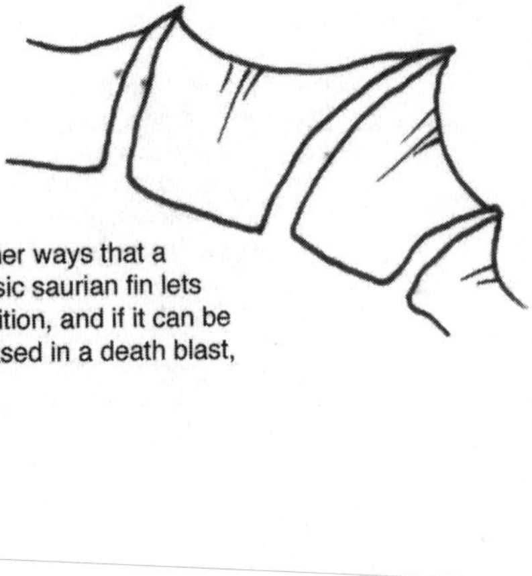

Aside from spikes, there are a number of other ways that a Giant Monster can be decked out. The classic saurian fin lets others know that you have a respect for tradition, and if it can be used to harness cosmic radiation to be released in a death blast, all the better.

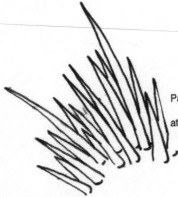

Patches of hairy spines can accent different parts of a monster and make grappling uncomfortable for attackers. They can also say, "Hey, look, I have weird patches of hairy-looking spines on my body, all from eating nuclear waste!"

HOW TO DRAW MANGA

Giant Monsters

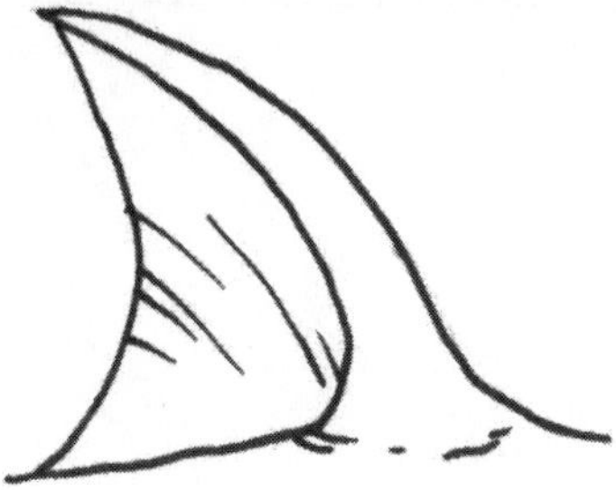

An aquatic fin will help any Giant Monster swim better, and some of them can excrete paralyzing venom, which is a nice perk.

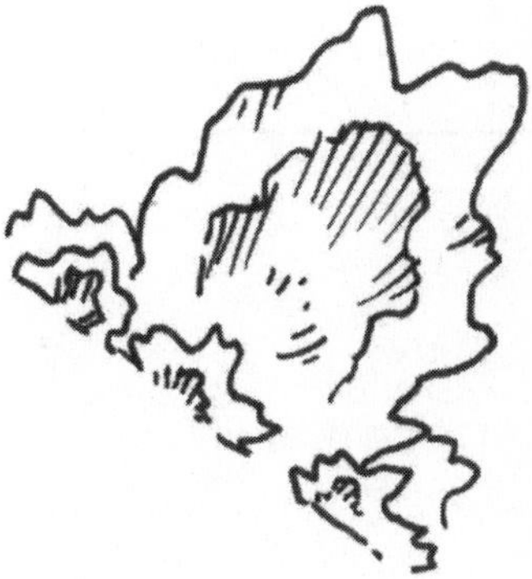

Weathered bone plates can make all kinds of statements, like, "Hey, I spend a lot of time in the ocean and let things grow on me," or "Look, I'm old."

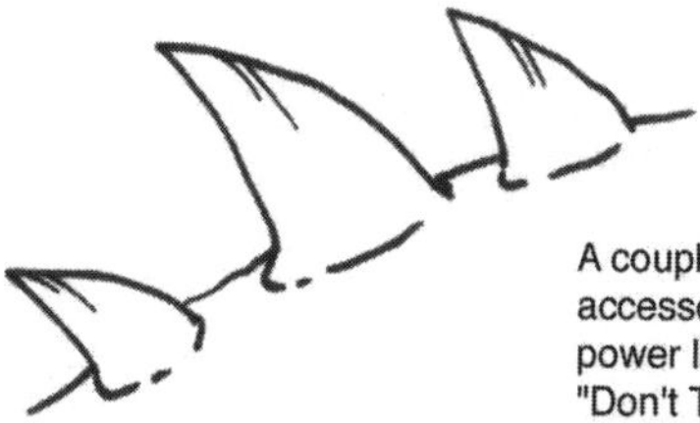

A couple of bone spurs are the bare minimum for any accessorized Giant Monster. You can hang trees and power lines from them, and they are great at saying, "Don't Touch!"

HOW TO DRAW MANGA

Giant Monsters

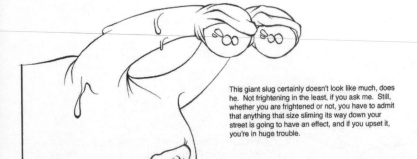

This giant slug certainly doesn't look like much, does he. Not frightening in the least, if you ask me. Still, whether you are frightened or not, you have to admit that anything that size sliming its way down your street is going to have an effect, and if you upset it, you're in huge trouble.

HOW TO DRAW MANGA

Giant Monsters

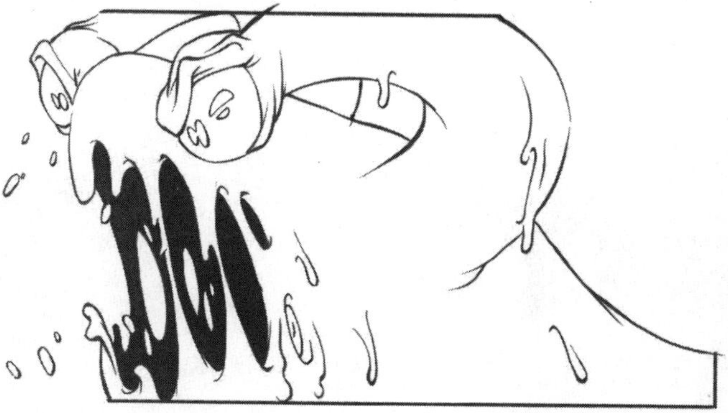

See! What did I tell you about upsetting a 200-ton slug? Do you have any idea how hard it is to get slug slime out of Main Street?

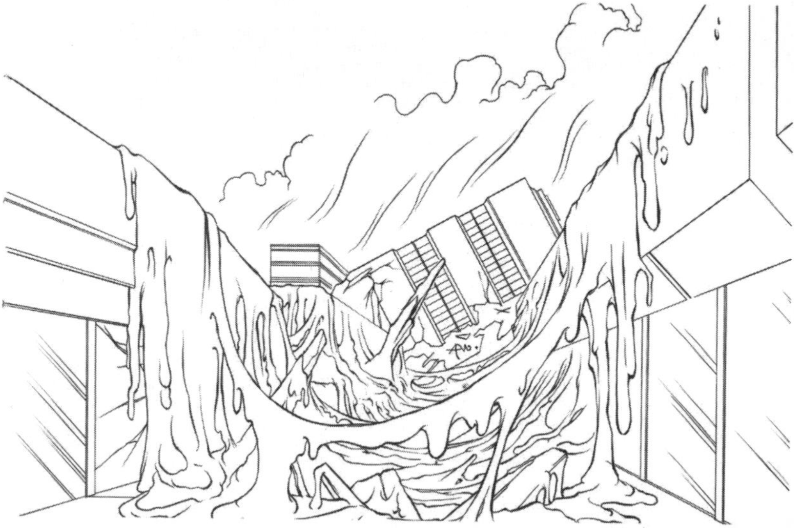

HOW TO DRAW MANGA
Giant Monsters

When a giant monster is created by humans, you are pretty much assured that you are in for a rough ride. This monster was the result of a scientist attempting to place his consciousness into a large body of water. It worked. Oh, the joys of modern science. Sadly, the strain of holding himself together has worn this scientist down, and since every time he tries to get close to his machines he shorts them out, he has become pretty agitated. Here's hoping another giant monster with a huge thirst comes along and deals with him, or else this living tidal wave may flood the neighborhood.

One of the nice things about drawing gigantic monsters is that it is okay if the little people have little or no detail. When a monster is truly giant, he will be too big to notice or care about any detail. The key is to get across these three ideas: fleeing, peril, and panic.

HOW TO DRAW MANGA

Giant Monsters

A giant, shapeless blob can be pretty dangerous, especially when its body is composed of a flesh-digesting jelly and it needs to consume hundreds of thousands of calories a day. There isn't really any place you can hide from a monster that is capable of oozing through the smallest cracks or, when that fails, simply digesting its way through any obstacle. Great origins for monsters like this include outer space, deep beneath the Earth's crust, and your mother's uncleaned garbage disposal.

Notice how even the clothing is digested. This is an economical monster, wasting nothing. Ain't nature neat?

HOW TO DRAW MANGA

Giant Monsters

This giant monster is dedicated to ruining your beach time. A monster without eyes, a nose, or ears and with a huge mouth is probably only concerned with one thing: eating, and after that, eating some more. The double row of teeth means he is twice as focused on food. This monster would probably fall into the "other" group.

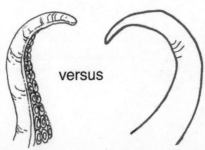

This monster is interesting in that it has tentacles and seems to originate from the ocean.

versus

Instead of having suckers, its tentacles are covered in the same skin as the rest of its body. This probably means that this creature can't afford to have any soft skin on its body.

HOW TO DRAW MANGA

Giant Monsters

Less of a giant monster and more of a giant problem, swarm attacks are no laughing matter. In some respects, the hive is the giant monster, and when it acts with a single mind, it can be more deadly than any single large creature. A hive of killer bees can kill a person with rapidity and ease. A swarm of locusts will devour everything and anything in its path. Ants on a rampage will not only eat everything, they will knock down things that are in their way. Add a little toxic leakage or radioactive mutation, and you are dealing with a situtation that is no small problem.

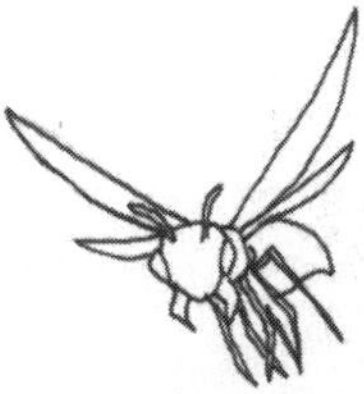

One bee alone is a nuisance. 300,000 is unholy retribution.

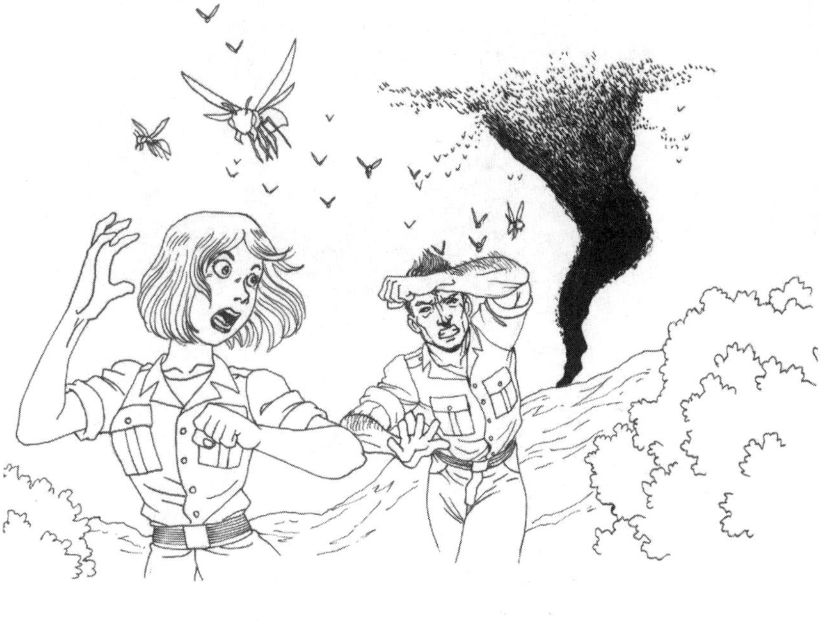

HOW TO DRAW MANGA
Giant Monsters

Sometimes Giant Monsters seem limited from a storytelling point of view. The immediate conclusion is that rampaging and destroying a city is all they are good for. Nothing could be further from the truth, as the continued survival of the genre can attest.

A Giant Monster's motivation is almost always a mystery, because it cannot communicate with humans. The chance exists that a Giant Monster is actually benevolent, but because of its nature it is attacked, or it might simply be a foil, its presence being the catalyst for an entirely different story. One of the most visually exciting ideas is multiple Giant Monsters fighting each other and humans being merely bystanders, seeking to understand what they are witnessing.

It is important to try and capture both the terror and sheer magnitude of Giant Monsters as well as their majesty and awe-inspiring nature.

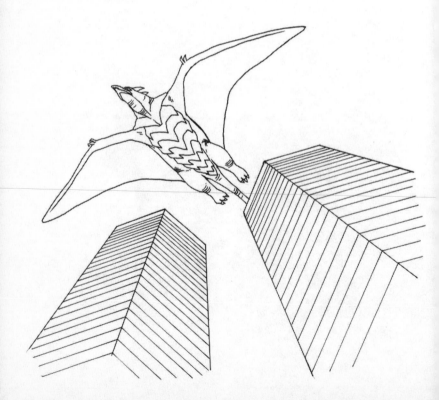

PRACTICE PAGE

ANIMAL LAND MECHA

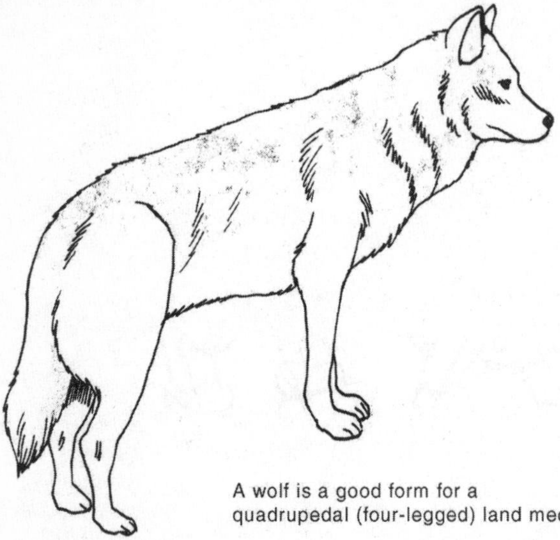

A wolf is a good form for a quadrupedal (four-legged) land mech.

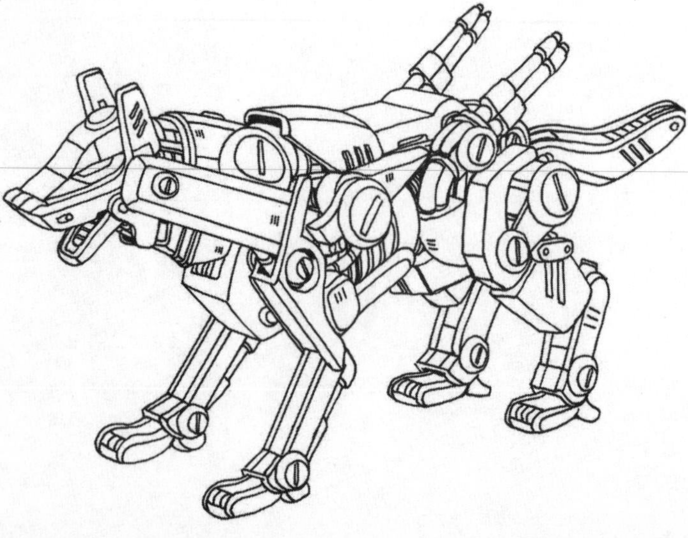

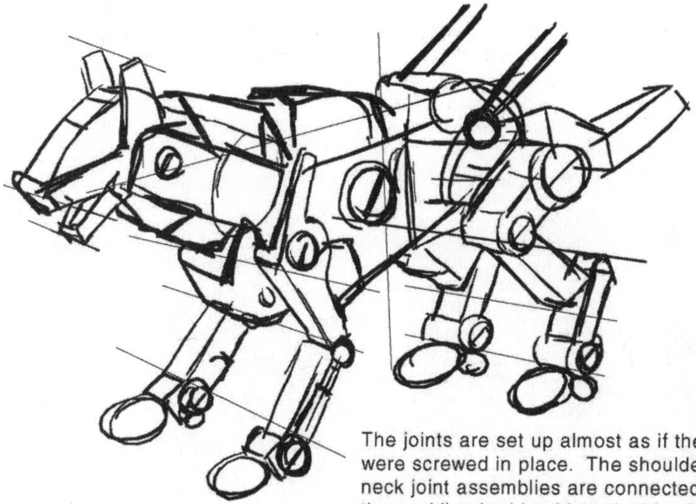

The joints are set up almost as if they were screwed in place. The shoulder and neck joint assemblies are connected, and the neckline is ridged into the shoulder.

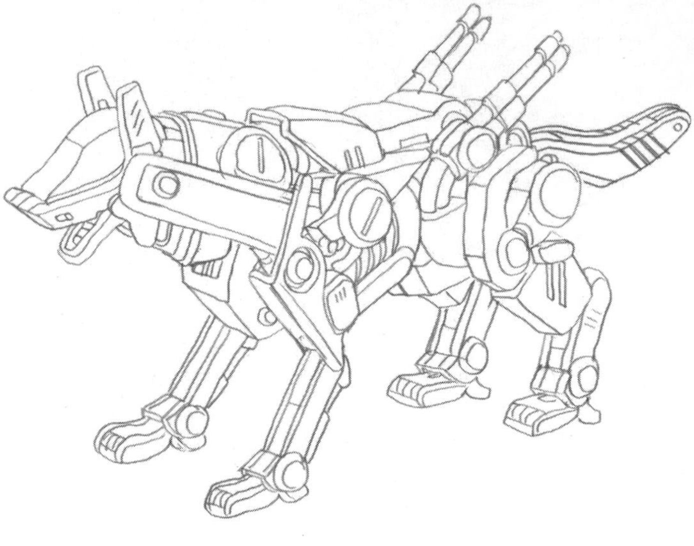

Mecha

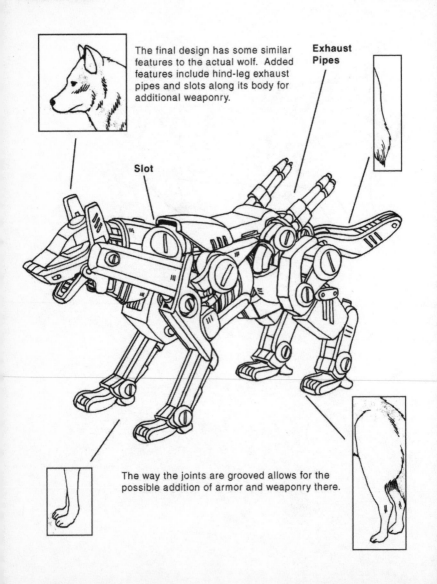

The final design has some similar features to the actual wolf. Added features include hind-leg exhaust pipes and slots along its body for additional weaponry.

Exhaust Pipes

Slot

The way the joints are grooved allows for the possible addition of armor and weaponry there.

**ANIMAL
SEA
MECHA**

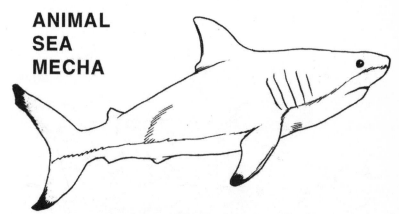

The shark is a killing machine and a perfect
example for a sea-based mech.

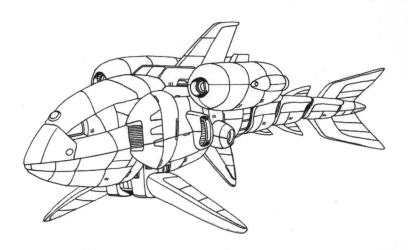

HOW TO DRAW MANGA
Mecha

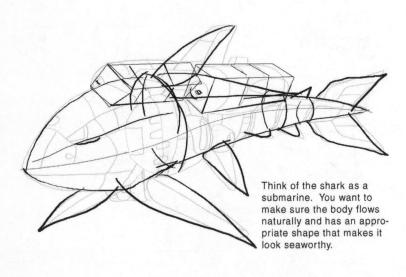

Think of the shark as a submarine. You want to make sure the body flows naturally and has an appropriate shape that makes it look seaworthy.

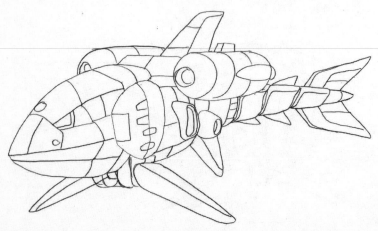